POLITICAL
THEOLOGY

POLITICAL
THEOLOGY

DOROTHEE SOELLE

Translated and with an Introduction by

JOHN SHELLEY

FORTRESS PRESS
Philadelphia

Contents

Introduction

by JOHN SHELLEY

Since the publication in 1965 of her first book, *Christ the Representative: An Essay in Theology after the "Death of God*,"[1] Dorothee Soelle has emerged as one of the most creative and controversial young theologians in Germany today. Her clear poetic style, which avoids as much as possible the technical jargon of academic theology, has made her thought accessible to a broad spectrum of readers—professors and students, clergy and laity.[2] She is among the few who have been able to make theology a topic of public conversation.

But perhaps even more controversial than Soelle's writings has been her role in initiating and leading the "Politisches Nachtgebet" in Cologne, West Germany,[3] a work

1. *Stellvertretung: Ein Kapitel Theologie nach dem "Tode Gottes"* (Stuttgart: Kreuz Verlag, 1965). English edition, trans. David Lewis (Philadelphia: Fortress, 1967).
2. Soelle's outstanding literary success is attested by the popularity of her books. For example, *Stellvertretung* is now in its sixth German edition and has been translated into five languages; and *Phantasie und Gehorsam* (Stuttgart: Kreuz Verlag, 1968) sold over 40,000 copies in its first edition.
3. See *Politisches Nachtgebet in Köln*, ed. Dorothee Soelle and Fulbert Steffensky, 2 vols. (Stuttgart/Mainz: Kreuz/Grünewald, 1971). These volumes contain a brief introduction to the group, a statement of its objectives, a large collection of worship services, and a sampling of public responses to the services. The title means literally "political evening prayer."

group searching for concrete ways of bringing faith and praxis together. Meetings in the form of "political" worship services are held once a month and focus on a particular theme or problem of immediate political or social interest, e.g., the Russian invasion of Czechoslovakia in 1968, American involvement in Vietnam, economic discrimination in West Germany. Typically the service begins with a very detailed description and analysis of the problem and is followed by a scripture reading, a brief address, prayer, and a discussion of "What can we do?" The group has probably elicited more denunciation than praise from the public, and certainly from the established church, but its influence has begun to spread and similar groups have sprung up in at least twelve cities in Germany and Switzerland.

But despite her outstanding literary success and the continuing influence of the Politisches Nachtgebet, Soelle does not enjoy the professional recognition, even in Germany, that she would seem to deserve. Born in 1929 in Cologne, she studied classical philology and philosophy at the university there before moving to the study of theology and Germanic philology at Göttingen and Freiburg. At Göttingen, where she finished her dissertation ("Investigations into the Structure of the Night Vigil in Bonaventura") in 1959, her teachers were Friedrich Gogarten and Ernst Käsemann. After six years as a high school teacher of German and religion and two more as an assistant at the Philosophical Institute of the University of Aachen, she moved back to the University of Cologne where she currently teaches in the Institute of Germanic Philology. But her dominant interest remains theology, as evidenced by all of her publications. Given her credentials, one cannot help but wonder why she has never been offered a position on a theology faculty. Is it because she is a woman? Or is it due to her penetrating critique of the religious establishment and the bourgeois ideology that she finds concealed in its theological dogmas?

In England and the United States Soelle has remained a virtual unknown, completely overshadowed by her male contemporaries—Moltmann, Metz, and Pannenberg. Three of her works have already been translated into English,[4] but none could be considered a literary success. This may be due to several factors. For one thing, these three English translations have all been published by different presses, and variations in orthography (Sölle, Soelle, or Solle) have often created confusion as to her identity. Furthermore, Soelle's first book, *Christ the Representative*, was reviewed in few American journals, and so far as I know is cited in significant fashion by only two American scholars.[5] British reviewers, possibly misled by the subtitle (*An Essay in Theology after the "Death of God"*) and the intentional ambiguities in Soelle's use of the phrase "death of God," tended—mistakenly, I think—to interpret the book entirely in the context of the American "Death of God" movement, and that label unfortunately has continued to stick.

4. In addition to *Christ the Representative* these are: *The Truth Is Concrete*, trans. Dinah Livingstone (New York: Herder & Herder, 1969); *Beyond Mere Obedience: Reflections on a Christian Ethic for the Future*, trans. Lawrence W. Denef (Minneapolis: Augsburg, 1970).

5. See Peter C. Hodgson, *Jesus—Word and Presence* (Philadelphia: Fortress, 1971), pp. 10–13, 18–19, 64, 242–243; and Leander E. Keck, *A Future for the Historical Jesus* (Nashville/New York: Abingdon, 1971), pp. 170–173, 176, 199.

Although Soelle clearly wants to avoid the narrow personalism and individualism that has been characteristic of many existentialist thinkers, *Christ the Representative* is better understood against the background of contemporary existentialism. The overarching question, at least, is the existentialist question *par excellence*: "How can one achieve personal identity?" The answers of traditional theism are no longer adequate, for a supernatural God is no longer a part of our immediate experience, and the traditional answers cannot deal with the technological axiom that everything is interchangeable and therefore replaceable. Modern man thus lives in the tension between the quest for personal identity, the fragmented experience of his own uniqueness and irreplaceability, and the technological principle that he, like everything else, is interchangeable. Soelle proposes a synthesis—man is irreplaceable, yet representable—and thus seeks to revive the ancient christological title of "representative" as a way of answering the identity question in our own time. Thus Soelle does share with the American death of God theologians the experience of the absence of God, the fact that he is no longer a part of our immediate experience, but she does not share their optimism that man can achieve his identity without God. To be sure Soelle does seem to equivocate as to whether this experience of absence is simply a psychosocial phenomenon of the last two centuries or whether it is an affirmation that God has not yet come in the fullness of his identity. But it is clear that Jesus is not intended to be a God-substitute; Jesus "represents" God but does not replace him. He is both identical and non-identical with God. In any case, and especially in light of her more recent writings, it seems that the christological category of "representation" is not merely a way of interpreting God's absence but, paradoxically, also a way of affirming his presence. Hence it is not God who is dead, but theism, the belief in a God who intervenes supernaturally in the causal nexus of the world. Precisely this death of theism is the foundation of Soelle's *Political Theology*.

"Political theology," especially in the German discussion, has become an explosive term; it is beset with ambiguities and burdened by a long and controversial history. Many view it as a contradiction of terms, but often for very different reasons. Some insist that theology can never be "political," because the church—and therefore theology—must rise above political and social strife if it is to fulfill its true mission of reconciliation.[6] Others, especially the young Marxists, see political theology as an anachronism, because in their view theology is simply an antiquated ideology offering nothing of value to modern political science.[7]

Historically, of course, political theology has been identified with a theological metaphysic that gave religious sanction to existing social and political structures. The term itself can be traced to Stoicism, but even the Greek city

6. For example, see Hans Maier, *Kritik der politischen Theologie* (Einsiedeln: Johannes Verlag, 1970), pp. 16–22.
7. The relation of political theology to Marxism is ambivalent. For Marx himself, theology was an ideological superstructure that served bourgeois interests, and there could be no rapprochement between theology and politics. Political theology, on the other hand, has learned much from Marxist thought and it is concerned to develop and refine the Marxist critique of religion and society. It breaks decisively with Marxism, however, in its contention that only theology, which has the power to be self-critical, can prevent this critique from dissolving into a new ideology.

states of an earlier period were founded on a political religion, the function of which was to insure domestic tran-
quillity and prosperity by appeasing the gods.[8] This concept
was developed further in imperial Rome until finally the
state itself became an object of worship. It was precisely
this type of pagan political theology or national religion
that was the target of Augustine's devastating attack in *The
City of God*. But Augustine's warnings went unheeded and
Christianity frequently assumed the role of a political religion, thus initiating a cordial alliance between church and
state that remained virtually intact until the Enlightenment,
when Christianity was first recognized to be historically,
socially, and politically conditioned. The Enlightenment—
and later the Marxist—critique of religion dealt a damag-
ing blow to political theology. But instead of dealing constructively with the critique, the mainstream of theology
took leave of the sociopolitical sphere and retreated to the
inner world of the individual. Thus began the trend toward
the privatization of religion.

The new political theology[9] is first of all a critical theology and not one that naïvely sanctions the existing sociopolitical order. Its roots lie in the Enlightenment, which is

8. See Hans Schmidt, "Politics and Christology: Historical Background," in *Faith and the World of Politics*, ed. J. B. Metz, *Concilium*, vol. 36 (New York: Herder and Herder, 1968), pp. 72–84.
9. In the 1930s political theology was the subject of a lively debate
between Carl Schmitt (*Politische Theologie* [Berlin: Duncker &
Humblot, 1922] and Erik Peterson (*Der Monotheismus als politisches Problem: Ein Beitrag zur Geschichte der politischen Theologie
in Imperium Romanum* [Leipzig: Jakob Hegmer, 1935]), the latter
concluding that Christianity has broken with political theology once
and for all. There the matter rested until 1968 when J. B. Metz re-
vived the term but with a new meaning. See Metz, *Theology of the
World*, trans. William Glen-Doepel (New York: Herder & Herder,
1969), pp. 107–124.

precisely the point at which the old political theology dis-
integrated. Theology has long since recognized the value
and necessity of historical criticism, and to this extent it has
been a true child of the Enlightenment. But the Enlightenment criticism of religion was not confined to mere historical considerations, for with equal passion it probed ideological and sociological dimensions as well. In its preoccupation
with the private individual, however, theology has all but
ignored these aspects of criticism.

This emphasis on a critical theology forms the basis of
Soelle's contention that political theology is best understood
in the context of Rudolf Bultmann's existentialist theology
(the German edition of this book bears the subtitle, "A
Conversation with Rudolf Bultmann"). Bultmann, according to Soelle, is one of the few theologians who has been
able to appropriate the historical-critical method in a constructive fashion. The logic of that method, which has its
roots in the Enlightenment, as applied by Bultmann leads to
political theology and not to "kerygmatic neoorthodoxy,"
which has become his heir apparent. It has frequently been
pointed out, for example, that form criticism is as much a
sociological method as an historical method, which suggests
some kind of interdependence between theology and the
social milieu.[10] But in actual practice the sociological aspects of the method are almost always confined to antiquity
—to the first-century church—and are rarely applied to the
modern situation. The point is that theology, whether it be
of the first century or the twentieth, cannot be isolated from

10. See Jürgen Moltmann, "Theologische Kritik der politischen Religion," in *Kirche im Prozess der Aufklärung,* ed. J. B. Metz, J. Moltmann, and W. Oelmüller (Mainz/Munich: Chr. Kaiser/Grünewald,
1970), pp. 14–15.

the social, political, and economic spheres. Thus the question of meaning—What do we mean when we speak of God?—must be supplemented by the more practical question: What are the social and political consequences of speaking of God, or remaining silent, in a particular situation?[11]

The critical function of political theology has been variously described. Metz refers to it as the "deprivatizing of theology,"[12] whereas Moltmann and Frederick Herzog speak of awakening the political consciousness of theology.[13] The disintegration of the old political theology and the trend toward privatization have fostered the illusions of an apolitical church and an apolitical theology, that is, a church and theology totally independent of social and political considerations. But there is no pure ecclesiastical neutrality, just as there is no apolitical theology; there are only those who are conscious of their political assumptions and consequences and those who are not. Hence it is not a matter of purging theology and the church of all social and political implications, but of bringing such implications to the attention of theology and encouraging it to reflect critically and responsibly on them.

The critical task of political theology has provoked only minor dissent among its proponents. The constructive task, however, is just beginning, and it is here that the real problems—and pitfalls—of political theology begin to emerge.

11. Ibid., p. 16.

12. Metz, *Theology of the World*, p. 110.

13. Jürgen Moltmann, "Political Theology," *Theology Today*, 28 (April 1971): 7–9. Frederick Herzog, "Political Theology in the American Context," *Theological Markings*, 1 (Spring 1971): 28–42.

Dorothee Soelle is one of the few who has begun to struggle with these problems, and her contributions to the constructive task make the present volume the best available introduction to political theology. Thus Soelle not only helps to locate political theology within the spectrum of contemporary options; she also elucidates the complex issues that confront a constructive political theology and begins to wrestle with them in a very creative fashion. Although a thorough and technical analysis is out of place in this summary introduction, it may be helpful to enumerate some of these issues, giving brief attention to Soelle's own contributions.

The problem of revelation in a political theology is tied directly to ideological criticism, which Soelle views as an instrument of self-criticism for theology; it is the means by which the absolute basis of theology—the gospel or kerygma—is freed from its ideological fixations. The need for ideological criticism is demonstrated very clearly, but the methodology needs to be developed more fully, especially with regard to the norms or standards by which it is carried out. To put it in the form of a question: What prevents political theology from becoming just another political ideology?

What is the conception of God in a political theology? Soelle has moved from traditional theism via the death of God to the "God of the oppressed," but beyond that the conception remains vague, leaving many unanswered questions. What is the ontological status of this post-theistic "God of the oppressed"? For example, does he enjoy personal agency and by what means does he act in history?

Political theology is currently lacking a full-blown philosophical anthropology (such as that which Bultmann appropriated from Heidegger), and this poses real problems for a political hermeneutic. Soelle, drawing heavily from Hegel and Marx and the social sciences, has sketched the basic features of a political anthropology, which contrasts sharply with the individualistic and personalistic emphases of existentialism. She sees human existence as constituted by the contradiction between one's experience of being determined by biological, cultural, and social forces on the one hand and one's experience of himself as an "I" (the experience of freedom) on the other. It is just this contradiction that drives man to transform the world in which he lives, that gives him the potential of becoming a *cooperator Dei*. But until the conception of God is elucidated more fully, that too remains unclear.

Traditional preoccupation with sin as pride, achievement, etc., encourages a sense of powerlessness (I myself can do nothing!) and abdication of responsibility. Soelle's lucid analysis of sin as collaboration and apathy (see Chapter 7) provides a very discerning understanding of the social dimension of sin, but without eroding one's sense of responsibility. However, it is not clear whether this is intended to replace or merely complement the more traditional interpretations of sin. If the former, then one must ask whether this understanding is sufficient to account for the experience of radical evil.

Political theology may signal a renewal of interest in the Jesus of history, whom Soelle discovers to be the political Jesus. She does not mean that he was a Zealot or a political revolutionary, but rather that he engaged in a ministry of "liberation." This becomes the link between Jesus' ministry and our own, even though we necessarily have a much broader understanding of liberation because of advances in the social sciences. However, this attempt to ground political theology in the New Testament seems a bit premature, and a more thorough exegetical foundation is needed.

The traditional Protestant understanding of forgiveness as something that happens primarily between God and the individual tends to divorce forgiveness from man's responsibility for the world. Soelle is able to show (see Chapter 8) how a political understanding of man and world leads to a broader understanding of forgiveness that is not only inseparable from responsibility but is also socially mediated. But here again the lack of a developed doctrine of God leads to some confusion. For example, has the horizontal dimension of forgiveness completely supplanted the vertical? If that is the case, then has God himself not become superfluous?

Eschatology plays a major role in a political theology, for the eschatological promise nourishes the hope for sociopolitical renewal within history. But the dialectical structure of this relation between history and eschatology remains undeveloped. One might ask the question this way: How can eschatological images function in a political theology without being identified as a political order officially sanctioned by Christianity?

It is with a genuine sense of gratitude that I acknowledge the many ways in which people have contributed to this translation project. In particular, I must mention Professor Peter Hodgson, my dissertation advisor at Vanderbilt University who graciously consented to serve as consultant for the project. He patiently plodded through the entire manuscript with the German text in hand, and his suggestions improved the style and the accuracy of the translation. His wife Eva was a great help with the more difficult passages, and a final reading of the manuscript by Professor Sallie TeSelle led to several last minute refinements. The author herself responded promptly and completely to questions about the book. Finally, I owe a special thank you to my wife Anne, who helped in a number of ways, and to my son Mark, who was never too busy to play with me when I needed a break from the rigors of academic pursuits.

Foreword

This book grew out of a lecture on Bultmann's hermeneutical method and political theology, which I delivered in Hofgeismar at the theological conference of Old Marburgers on October 7, 1970. The ensuing discussion brought to light the essential difficulties of communication, and I should like to thank the participants of that conference, all of whom belong to the broader circle of friends and students of Rudolf Bultmann, for their criticism and provocative suggestions.

This approach to the subject contains a definite limitation. A political theology could be˙ developed far more directly from the early writings of Paul Tillich, who understood religious socialism as "the radical application of the prophetic-Protestant principle to religion and Christianity."[1] It might have been possible to avoid many a detour having little to do with political theology and more with German history of this century and the reception of theological thought that bears its peculiar stamp. But perhaps this detour—the conversation with a system of thought that understands itself as essentially apolitical—is important for

1. Paul Tillich, *Political Expectation,* ed. James L. Adams (New York: Harper & Row, 1971), p. 54.

the goal of a political theology, for it unites and reconciles what is apparently apolitical with the present social tasks of theology.

The second half of the book (Chapters 5–8) would have been inconceivable apart from the many conversations with friends from the ecumenical work group known as Politisches Nachtgebet in Cologne. Much that we thought about and hoped for in common and in controversy is further elaborated and reexamined from a theological perspective. To thank the work group would be inconsistent with our way of communicating with each other. But perhaps a thank you is included in this plea for further work toward politicizing the conscience of men and women in Cologne and elsewhere. I dedicate this book to Frieder Stichler, who lost his job because of political theology.[2]

Cologne, March, 1971   Dorothee Soelle

2. Cf. *akid* (*aktion kirchenreform informationsdienst*) 1/70.

1. From Existentialist to Political Theology

In a baptismal address sometime in May, 1944, Dietrich Bonhoeffer wrote to the coming generation:

> For you thought and action will enter on a new relationship; your thinking will be confined to your responsibilities in action. With us thought was often the luxury of the on-looker; with you it will be entirely subordinated to action.[1]

Has this prophecy been fulfilled? Have we really discovered a new relation between thought and action, between theory and praxis? Is it not the case that theological thinking has exempted itself from this necessity? What kind of praxis has it developed? What has it learned from praxis, even one that has accomplished nothing? In this connection Bonhoeffer cites one of Jesus' sayings from the Sermon on the Mount: "Not every one who says to me, 'Lord, Lord,' shall enter the kingdom of heaven, but he who does the will of my father who is in heaven" (Matt. 7:21)—a saying which the theologian can hear only as a critical question addressed to himself. Is not the whole of theology "Lord-

1. Dietrich Bonhoeffer, *Letters and Papers from Prison*, ed. Eberhard Bethge, trans. Reginald H. Fuller, and rev. Frank Clarke and others (3d English ed.; New York: Macmillan, 1967), p. 158.

1

Lord-talk," which is precisely a way of avoiding the will of God? In spite of its sincere efforts to be more worldly, does not theology still remain locked in its ivory tower of Lord-Lord-talk?

The answer to this question will have to be given in our generation. The theological program that must be undertaken is called "political theology"—specifically one that understands itself not as a mere component but as the essential formulation of the theological problem for our time. This book is an attempt to work at such a program, specifically in the form of a critical conversation with the theology of Rudolf Bultmann. It is at the same time an attempt to take account of its distinctive theological roots and to relate them to the next stage of political theology, which seeks to bring faith and action together more satisfactorily. The conversation will lead to points of agreement and disagreement with the thought of Bultmann, but not merely for biographical or accidental reasons. More and more it appears to me that the move from existentialist theology to political theology is itself a consequence of the Bultmannian position. Certainly today there are various points of departure and methods that lead to a political theology. The political involvement of the Christian almost goes without saying in the sphere of Karl Barth's theology. The accent shifts, however, depending upon whether one begins with revelation, with promise, or with a hermeneutical circle that explicitly includes the situation and context of the political question. It may be precisely the historico-critical consciousness that is destined to develop a politico-critical consciousness. Moreover, the critical rationality honed in the demythologizing debate could become important for a political theology, because it can guard against the utopian tendency inherent in political theology to avoid reality.

But precisely that is the point at issue. Is there after all a bridge between existentialist and political thought? Are the existentialist and political interpretations of the gospel not mutually exclusive? Have they anything in common? Theologically speaking, does the one necessarily follow from the other? What is the relation of Bultmann's hermeneutic to a political theology, both that with established foundations as well as one that may be developed in the future? How are historical criticism and ideological criticism related as to awareness of the problem, formulation of the question, practical method, and, ultimately, results? How do we move from a theology whose key words are "faith" and "understanding" to one which focuses on faith and action?

The sociological study by Goldschmidt and Spiegel, *Der Pfarrer in der Grosstadt* (1969), concludes that pastors who embrace the theology of Bultmann place greater emphasis on the formation of political opinion within their congregations and on the public responsibility of faith than do church officials with more conservative theological ties. How is this fact to be interpreted? If we search for the common ground shared by historical-critical theology and political consciousness, we discover that both have the same positive relation to the Enlightenment, to "man's coming of age" (Kant). If we proceed on the assumption that the Enlightenment, as a process of coming of age, is indivisible, that is, that the specific critical capacities of men are not permitted to dictate the objects to which they apply, then

politically enlightened consciousness has descended from
the same critical, rational frame of mind to which theological enlightenment is indebted.

A positive relation to the Enlightenment is not to be
understood as one that remains blind to its consequences
and renders harmless those dialectical reversals that impose
a new and different form of enslavement precisely where
the bonds of a former servitude have been broken. Again
and again the risk that accompanies enlightenment must be
consciously accepted anew, even and precisely in theology.
The price of coming of age remains high: destruction of
traditional ties, insecurity and doubt, isolation and disap-
pointment. That this price is to be paid is for an enlightened
Christian, such as Lessing, a question of "confidence" in the
truth that needs no authoritative supports from without.
The unenlightened, timid Christian "can mean very well
with his religion, but he ought to trust it more"[2]—trust it, in
other words, to cleanse itself of superfluous embellishment
by means of a critical examination and thereby prove itself
to be true. As long as liberation and emancipation remain
the goal, enlightened criticism is not merely optional but a
necessary method. This goal is anticipated in the methodical
steps of criticism—of enlightenment—even when we recognize that the dialectic of progress redefines that goal again
and again. The fact that liberation has not yet been attained
is not an argument against it. There is no way that this fact

2. G. E. Lessing, *Zur Geschichte und Litteratur*, 4. Beitrag, 1777 Cf.
also Lessing, *Anti-Goeze*, 1778: "What? Because I trust the Christian
religion more than you, should I be branded an enemy of Christianity?
Because I report to the board of health the poison that creeps in the
darkness, should I be held responsible for bringing the plague into
the land?"

can serve as an alibi for those who want to reduce theological enlightenment to a mere instrumental, text-critical method and segregate it from political enlightenment.

Historical criticism of tradition and sociological criticism of institutions went hand in hand in the early period of the Enlightenment.[3] Criticism of the Bible was at the same time an attack on the power of the clergy. "Or do you think, Herr Hauptpastor, that it does not matter what the intellectuals believe in secret as long as the general public persists along the traditional ruts in which the clergy knows how to guide them? Do you believe that?"[4] Emancipation means criticism of the tradition and its guardians. But does this liberating intention of the critical consciousness also hold true for the theology of Rudolf Bultmann? What is its relation to general enlightenment? Does Bultmann's thought belong to the movement of the modern emancipation of man from unknown powers, whether they be mythically experienced or explained mythologically? If we assume we can answer this question affirmatively for the program of demythologizing that has emerged from the historical-critical method, what about existentialist interpretation? Does it represent a stage in the process of man's coming of age? Is it not frequently regarded today as a venture that has supported authoritarian, irrational, decisionist tendencies in our society and therefore as an instrument of counter-enlightenment? The question for Bultmann and for any theology is whether it makes men more capable of love, whether it encourages or obstructs the liberation of the individual and the commu-

3. Cf. Jürgen Moltmann, *Religion, Revolution, and the Future,* trans. M. Douglas Meeks (New York: Scribner's, 1969), pp. 84–85.
4. Lessing, *Anti-Goeze* (1778).

nity. Expressed scientifically, that is the verification principle; expressed biblically, the proof of the Spirit and of
power (1 Cor. 2:4). Thus the question raised for Bultmann's
theology concerns its openness to a political theology.

IDEOLOGICAL-CRITICAL METHODS

The methodologies that can lead to an answer to this
question are diverse. One possibility is the ideological-
critical method as it has been used in the Frankfurt School
and frequently applied to theology. In *Jargon der Eigentlichkeit* Adorno offers a critique of existentialist philosophy
oriented to its use of language. The theological validity of
the critique, especially with regard to Bultmann, is relatively unimportant, because the latter prefers scientific pre-
cision to jargon and is noticeably sparing in his appropriation of Heideggerian terminology, especially in regard to its
ideological-existentialist overtones. Bultmann borrows relatively few Heideggerian concepts, and even those few are
taken in a strict, highly formalized sense that is hardly concerned with content or even mood. Adorno can therefore
say: "Total demythologizing reduces transcendence entirely
to abstract concepts. Contrary to the desire of the obscuran-
tists, the Enlightenment, which they decry, triumphs in
their work." Now Bultmann cannot be considered an
obscurantist in the sense of these remarks if one considers
the role that dialectical theology has played in his thought,
a matter to which Adorno proceeds critically: "In the same
movement of mind, however, the veiled, established authority of the subject once again conjures up myth in the whole
of dialectical theology: the highest principle of the subject,

as absolutely different, is blind."[5] This theological criticism of Bultmann must still be discussed; however, the critique of language concerning the jargon of authenticity does not apply to Bultmann himself, but it certainly does to the rampant jargon of kerygma.

Within the scope of this critique of language and ideology fall those attempts to criticize Bultmann by bringing his theology into a confrontation with political reality. A criticism of a Marburg sermon of December 14, 1939, published in the journal *Kritischer Katholizismus* should serve as a good example. The basic thrust of the case against Bultmann runs as follows: renunciation of information, deficiency of concrete ideas, appeal to the contemplation instead of the rationality of the hearer, equivocation between language on a real and on a metaphorical plane. The major criticism is circumscribed under the category of "derealization," a psychological term that characterizes abnormal states in which the perception and understanding of reality is distorted or entirely destroyed. "The war becomes the occasion for demonstrating the necessity of a joy that cannot exist under actual conditions" and whose "otherworldly quality is achieved at the price of the loss of reality." The otherworldly joy is unmasked as "an ideal superstructure of a hopeless reality," the spirit of resistance is extinguished, and God himself is placed at the service of existing conditions. The appropriate hearers of such a sermon would be disciplined, patient Christians, who represented, in the opinion of the critic, no serious threat to the

5. T. W. Adorno, *Jargon der Eigentlichkeit* (Frankfurt: Suhrkamp, 1964), pp. 29–30.

Nazis. The upshot of all this is: "Thus even the existentialist interpretation with its exclusive interest in the individual and the possibility of authentic existence plays indirectly into the hands of Fascism."[6] To be sure, this critical voice from the younger generation deserves our attention, for it poses very sharply the problem raised by Bultmann's other-worldly tendencies.

But it appears to me that the criticism is inappropriate for two reasons: First, there is lacking here an historical consciousness that recalls the conditions of life under a dictatorship; and second, it seems to me fallacious to level this charge on a sermon, because the field on which the Bultmannian theology can be tested is not the sermons of Rudolf Bultmann. The sermon as a rhetorical-literary type has a surprising inertia, a strongly traditional and, especially for Bultmann, a narrowly individual character. It is not difficult at all to criticize traditional sermons from the standpoint of a progressive social consciousness (which is in no way shared by the community of churchgoers). This criticism of Bultmann, with its important points of dereal-ization in the face of suffering and training in political obedience and patience, could become of interest to theology if it were applied to the theology of Bultmann and if the characteristic features found in his sermons were in fact also found at the core of Bultmann's theology. I have cited this article in detail to emphasize the existential motivation for the criticism of Bultmann. Whether it is correct, whether the repression of suffering and the incapacity of mourning, which seek their theological justification in the *hōs mē* (1

6. M. Hermanns, "Wie progressiv sind unsere Progressiven? 3. Rudolf Bultmann," *Kritischer Katholizismus* (July 1969).

Cor. 7:29–31), are really characteristic of Bultmann's theology remains to be determined. From a strictly methodological point of view this problem cannot be resolved by focusing on the periphery of Bultmann's thought, that is, on random, isolated remarks about politics or on sermons. It can be resolved only internally, and that means with the aid of critical questions concerning the essentially new theological knowledge of Bultmann himself.

2. The Historical-Critical Method

Viewed from a theological-historical perspective, the synthesis that Bultmann has effected is called "existentialist interpretation." It is developed from three very different elements (see the diagram on p. 38): first, the historical critical exegesis of the New Testament; second, the dialectical theology of the early 1920s; and finally—not so much as material content but certainly as a formal instrument—the philosophy of existence, without which a synthesis between the first two mutually exclusive theological perspectives would not have been possible for Bultmann.

CRITICISM AS THEOLOGICAL EMANCIPATION

Today it appears urgently necessary to expound the significance of the historical-critical method for Bultmann's theology, especially in view of the recurring tendency to subsume the theology of the twenties, Bultmann and Barth, under the rubric of a Word-of-God theology that obscures their differences—as though the decisive thing could be conveyed by this dogmatic slogan. Bultmann himself saw very early that the difference between Barth and himself lay precisely in the "internal relation to historical scholarship," a relation that he denies to Barth. In Bultmann's view, historical criticism is employed "not to establish causal de-

11

pendence, but rather in the service of self-reflection as the method of endless questioning," which leads ultimately to those questions that demand a decision of us.[1] Bultmann's roots in liberal theology, to which he was indebted, according to his own testimony, for the "development of the critical sense, i.e., of freedom and veracity," and without which he "could never have become or remained a theologian,"[2] were not suppressed later on by decisionism but were certainly modified by it. The theologically liberating import of the historical-critical method becomes clear when one realizes that, contrary to the dogmatic method, it is self-constituted. In the words of Ernst Troeltsch, the dogmatic method "proceeds from a fixed point completely removed from the relativity of history, and from that point of view attains unconditionally trustworthy propositions."[3]

In contrast to the dogmatic method, the historical method frees itself from the necessity of having to sacrifice critically acquired historical knowledge for the sake of the church's doctrinal tradition. According to its own projected goals, the historical criticism of the Bible is aimed at emancipation, which follows from the assumption still preserved in the first phase of the Enlightenment that reason and revelation intend the same thing, even if they represent two different approaches. On this enlightened horizon historical criticism can expose only the ephemeral dimension of the Bible and relativizes only the embellishments that are super-

1. *Karl Barth—Rudolf Bultmann: Briefwechsel, 1922–1966*, ed. B. Jaspert (Zürich: Theologischer Verlag, 1971), pp. 9–10. (letter to Barth of 12/31/22).

2. Rudolf Bultmann, *Faith and Understanding*, trans. Louise Pettibone Smith (New York: Harper & Row, 1969), 1:29.

3. Ernst Troeltsch, "Über historische und dogmatische Methode in der Theologie," cited by T. Lorenzmeier, "Zum Thema: Historischer Jesus," *Evangelische Kommentare*, 3 (1970): 297.

fluous to its claims. The faith prevails which declares that criticism could expound the truth of Scripture precisely in its liberating power. Bultmann clings to this original Enlightenment goal of historical criticism, even if this is no longer immediately apparent, for historical consciousness meanwhile has critically relativized not only the New Testament as the object of research, but even itself—which, on the model of that hermeneutical circle, is expressed concretely in critical reflection upon its own preunderstanding. Therefore the historical-critical method does not lead more directly to the truth of faith but, with the help of the self-reflection inherent in it, it poses for us the question of whether to decide for faith or for despair (in one of its many forms, such as skepticism or resignation).

The consciousness of method that has been developed in the course of the history of historical criticism is astonishing: literary criticism and poetic classification play as important a role as sociological methods, including sociology of knowledge, which are used in the literary criticism of the tradition. For example, the question of *Sitz-im-Leben* is none other than the question of the social conditions within which some oral traditions were preserved and passed on while others were forgotten. Which ethnic and religious groups transmitted and modified the tradition, and what kind of "cognitive structures" played a role in that process? To deny the sociological relevance of historical criticism would border upon an act of self-castration. Precisely when, as with Ebeling and for the sake of the whole hermeneutical process, one wishes to see the historical-critical method set free from the "curtailment to a mere technical tool,"[4]

4. Gerhard Ebeling, *Word and Faith*, trans. James W. Leitch (Philadelphia: Fortress, 1963), p. 49.

then neither the sociological nor the political relevance of this method may be bracketed out.

If form criticism instructs us, for example, that the individual pericopes of the Gospels were short sermons having the purpose of calling hearers to a decision, then it is not permissible to interpret this state of affairs in a merely personal way, because these sermons, indeed these public proclamations, were public scandals with political consequences for those concerned. In an essay entitled "Das politische Element in der historisch-kritischen Methode"[5] Josef Blank argues that criticism as such is a political factor, because it brings not only opinions and dogmas before the bar of reason but also the establishments and positions of power that in principle are bound up with them and supported by them. In this broad sense he perceives the basic element in criticism to be operative in the Bible itself in the religious, social, and political criticism carried on there. Even if this factor has not been taken over immediately by the historical-critical method, it still should not be overlooked that the biblical critics, as far as the historical Jesus is concerned, have taken their initiatives from the contradiction between his message and the dogmatic structures that it encountered.

DISPENSING WITH CRITICAL THOUGHT

At this point we must begin political theology's critique of existentialist theology, not specifically of Bultmann, but certainly of a limitation of historical criticism that contra-

---

5. Josef Blank, "Das politische Element in der historisch-kritischen Methode," in *Die Funktion der Theologie in Kirche und Gesellschaft*, ed. P. Neuenzeit (München: Kösel Verlag, 1969), pp. 39–60.

dicts its essence. The liberating significance of the historical-critical method is lost whenever one disregards the hermeneutical circle and subjects past texts to historical-critical examination, but not one's own present and its problematic character as reflected historically in its origin and its dependence on social and psychosocial factors. From the standpoint of the methodological consciousness of historical criticism, it is inconsistent to overlook either the conditions of one's own preunderstanding or the conditions of the self-understanding constituted by the encounter with the gospel. When understanding itself is conceived "as an ascent from socialization into the sphere of transcendent authentic existence,"[6] then no adequate fusion of horizons can take place between the past and present consciousness. When apparent constants from the New Testament world are introduced into our world without alteration, the historical-critical method is endangered by inconsistency.

The ahistorical interpretation of the oft-cited passage in Rom. 10:13 ff. represents an example of this deficiency of critical thought. In this passage Paul traces faith back to hearing, hearing to the sermon, and the sermon to the Word of Christ. Erich Grässer discovers in this text the "criterion of churchliness," namely, "unalterable structures" such as the sermon, and uses the Pauline text to justify existing church practice.[7] But surely even an unspecialized histori-

6. Helmut Peukert, ed., Introduction to *Diskussion zur "politischen Theologie"* (Mainz/Munich: Chr. Kaiser/Grünewald, 1969). p. viii.
7. Erich Grässer, "Die politische Herausforderung an die biblische Theologie," *Evangelische Theologie,* 30 (1970): 249, Methodologically, it is the same procedure—namely, dispensing with the historical-critical method—when Grässer approvingly cites Luther to justify the study of ancient languages for present-day students of theology: "For it is very risky to speak of God's Son otherwise or with other words than those which God himself uses."

cal scholarship, to say nothing of a formulation of the problem as worked out by sociology of knowledge, must seek to
clarify the *Sitz-im-Leben* of the Apostle. Paul's remarks concerning how men receive salvation presuppose the following data: (1) The New Testament, which in the future will
be the basis for all sermons, is at the time of these remarks
about preaching and hearing still in the process of being
formed; its parts are for the most part not yet written, and
in any case they have neither been edited nor collected and
canonized. (2) Even if a written document were under consideration, it would not essentially alter the preaching situation of Paul, because the majority of his hearers are
illiterate. (3) The general situation with respect to information is primitive, and therefore (compared to our situation) the curiosity or need for information is great. If one
neglects these data and translates the Pauline concept of
preaching into the present, contending that the church's
Sunday sermon is necessary for faith, then the wish may
have been the father of the idea.

I have given this example in detail to indicate a state of
affairs that is too little appreciated in the debates over
historical-critical method, namely, the distortion of Christian faith by Christian history. Representatives of the
historical-critical method are inclined to trivialize this history as far as hermeneutics is concerned, because they jump
directly from the twentieth century back to the first in an
attempt to bring to speech anew that which would be dis-
tinctively Christian irrespective of its historical mediation.
In fact, historical criticism has to do not only with just a
few things in the New Testament, such as mythological
representations that are to be interpreted or eliminated, but

also with apparently intelligible compositions in rational speech, such as the Pauline parenesis. Even abstract concepts like obedience, law, or sin demand an historical-critical analysis that clarifies what has been passed off under their name and what has been glossed over. The method laid out here leads from demythologizing, after a certain delay characteristic of theology, to ideological criticism in which not only the mythical residue but also the far more dangerous ideological structures of Christianity, which can be studied under the concept of obedience, are subjected to historical criticism.[8]

It is not enough to say, "The New Testament believes. . . ." We must show to what extent the gospel itself enables us to make a critique of Christian ideology. Similarly, whoever wants to proclaim the *solus Christus* cannot overlook the *Christus in ecclesia corruptus*. At this point it seems to me that the students' criticism of the "text-fetishism" of the exegetes is theologically justified in pursuit of the liberating claim of the historical-critical method. The historical-critical method is not threatened from without by an alleged "new wave" of scientific and historical hostility, but only by its own characteristic inconsistency, specifically in a threefold manner: first, because it limits itself and does not include present-day ecclesiastical and social structures and their ideological superstructures; second, because it overlooks the historical mediation of the contents of Christianity; and finally, because it exempts apparently invariable and always valid structures of faith and their appropriation. As long as historical criticism remains true to the Enlighten-

8. Cf. my book *Beyond Mere Obedience*, trans. Lawrence W. Denef (Minneapolis: Augsburg, 1970), pp. 81–85.

ment spirit in which it is grounded, which means asking
critically about historical mediations and conditions, and
as long as it preserves the essential features of any historical method (which according to Troeltsch are criticism,
analogy, and correlation) then not only does it have nothing to fear from a sociopolitical theology that is consciously
committed to the same methodological principles, but on the
contrary political theology carries on in the best tradition
of liberal theology and preserves precisely the methodological achievements of criticism, analogy, and correlation,
while enriching them with refinements from sociology and
sociology of knowledge.

3. Dialectical Theology

But is it true that the historical-critical method is really the foundation of Bultmannian theology? Has Bultmann held on to this assumption? Are not those persons correct who nowadays lump the theologies of Bultmann and Barth together under the common denominator of a Word-of-God theology? And is it not true that some of Bultmann's students have attained, in the concept of kerygma, an impregnable point that in principle is free precisely from criticism, analogy, and correlation—a point that can no longer be destroyed, relativized, or examined, since it denotes the Wholly Other, the unique and incomparable of the Christian faith? The second essential factor in Bultmann's synthesis is the early dialectical theology. It is difficult to assess properly its significance for Bultmann's thought, first because of changes in his thought itself, but also because of the eventual triumph of the Barthian orthodoxy that developed from dialectical theology in the kerygmatic-neoorthodox wing of the Bultmannian school. In the following pages I shall attempt to describe the influence of dialectical theology on Bultmann, first by discussing the "authority" of the text, then by examining the concept of kerygma as it was taken over by Bultmann in his critical appropriation of dialectical theology, and finally by considering the problem that arises with the renunciation of the historical Jesus.[1]

THE AUTHORITY OF THE TEXT

Bultmann begins with a criticism of the scientific method of reflection that exalts detached objectivity. Such a method interrogates the text for what it says as such (not for what it means for us today), disregarding its own point of view, which would be unscientific. Thus as we say today in the words of Lenin, such a method is unpartisan. Bultmann wants to move beyond objectivity as the ideal for the historical method of reflection, because he heeds the authority of texts. If today the expression *authority of the text* seems oppressive to us—denoting a voice that can be neither questioned nor criticized and that confronts us with an unavoidable claim—then we must attempt to understand this expression in its historical context. For Bultmann, that context has been provided by the overcoming of historicism and its manipulation of ancient texts as indifferent, value-free text-objects that are understood in a naturalistic way.[2]

1. For Bultmann's appropriation of dialectical theology, I am depending not so much on the early, emphatic essay of 1924 supporting Barth in the debate with Harnack—"Liberal Theology and the Latest Theological Movement" (in *Faith and Understanding*, trans. Louise Pettibone Smith [New York: Harper & Row, 1969], 1:28–52)—but more on the work of 1925, "The Problem of a Theological Exegesis of the New Testament" (in *The Beginnings of Dialectic Theology*, ed. James M. Robinson, [Richmond: John Knox, 1968], 1: 236–256), and above all on the lecture of 1927, "The Significance of 'Dialectical Theology' for the Scientific Study of the New Testament" (in *Faith and Understanding*, 1: 145–164).

2. For Bultmann the expression *authority* is formed in the context of antihistoricist polemic. When Schmithals speaks twenty-five years later of the "authoritative lordship of the Gospel," this mode of concept formation serves entirely different interests, for the opponent is now political theology. Cf. W. Schmithals, *Das Christuszeugnis in der heutigen Gesellschaft* (Hamburg: Herbert Reich, 1970), p. 13.

The authority of the text consists in its having to say something essentially new, because I cannot understand myself as a being who "is a priori thoroughly in control of all the possibilities which may be expressed."[3] That the text—and this means fundamentally any text—can become an event and is not a mere thing, is what constitutes its authority, which as a consequence is realized only in time. If it has nothing to say to me, if it does not add anything to my self-interpretation (the term Bultmann uses here before taking over Heidegger's concept of self-understanding), then its authority has been expended.

But what is the significance of this authority of the text for the question whether or not the liberating intention of the historical-critical method has been obscured by dialectical theology? The answer is found in the previously cited lecture of October, 1927 ("The Significance of 'Dialectical Theology' for the Scientific Study of the New Testament"), which goes much further in delimiting the place of dialectical theology within the system. Most important are two limitations imposed by Bultmann. First, he rejects a formalized dialectical method in which a proposition such as "God is merciful to the sinner" requires the dialectical opposite, "God is angry with the sinner." This way of thinking would be unsuitable for the New Testament, because it would lead one astray into ahistorical systematizing. The validity of the historical method remains undisputed, and the method itself is enriched by Bultmann's understanding of dialectical theology. The second limitation refers to dogmatic content. Bultmann protests here against a dogmatic usage of dialectical theology, as when certain dogmatic propositions such

3. Bultmann, "The Problem of a Theological Exegesis of the New Testament," *The Beginnings of Dialectic Theology,* p. 240.

as "eternity is not time," or "revelation and redemption are not historical," are made presuppositions for New Testament scholarship. Propositions of this sort, Bultmann contends, are only presumptive theological propositions,[4] because their relation to the subject matter is that of the detached observer who arranges a body of information, and that is precisely what Bultmann wants to overcome by his distinctive appropriation of dialectical theology. These are unhistorical propositions, supposedly always valid, independent of the situation, and deductively obtained.

The positive significance that Bultmann allots to dialectical theology is its "insight into the dialectic of existence, into the *historical nature of man's existence*." What he has learned from dialectical theology—or believes he has learned—is what he calls "the truth of temporal speech."

> Consequently a theological statement is not true because its content expresses something which is timelessly valid. It is true when it gives the answer to the question posed by the concrete situation in time to which the sentence itself belongs when it is being spoken.[5]

It appears to me that political theology, not kerygmatic neoorthodoxy, draws the logical conclusion from Bultmann's situational thinking, because it strives to hear precisely the questions posed by the current situation and to analyze them exactly, so that theologically "correct" answers are not handed out again and again as kerygma to questions that are not even being asked.

4. When similar propositions are coined by kerygmatic neoorthodoxy —e.g., "the royal lordship of Jesus Christ is the lordship of the Gospel, not of law" (Schmithals, *Das Christuszeugnis in der heutigen Gesellschaft*, p. 16.)—an appeal cannot be made to Bultmann because what is spoken of is a "concept" of the kingdom, not the kingdom itself.

5. Bultmann, *Faith and Understanding*, 1: 163–164, 147.

THE CONCEPT OF KERYGMA

When we analyze Bultmann's understanding of kerygma, we recover the formal structure typical of and necessary for his thought, which in itself is sufficient to vindicate him. Bultmann makes a fundamental distinction between kerygma and theology,[6] an important fact suppressed by the entire Bultmannian right. Kerygma appears "as a formidable summary of everything which has to be proclaimed, and now threatens to conceal the real problems facing proclamation under a welter of high-sounding christological terminology."[7] It becomes a collection of doctrines that can neither be criticized nor questioned, most of which—and this is deemed progress—are no longer formulated mythologically but ideologically.[8] By ideology I understand a system of propositional truths independent of the situation, a superstructure no longer relevant to praxis, to the situation, to the real questions of life. The superstructure has lost pre-

6. Ibid., p. 218.
7. Gerhard Ebeling, *Theology and Proclamation*, trans. John Riches (Philadelphia: Fortress, 1966), p. 36.
8. Cf. W. Schmithals, "Kein Streit um des Kaisers Bart: Zur Diskussion über das Bekenntnis zu Jesus Christus," *Evangelische Kommentare*, 3 (1970): 76–82. Schmithals speaks of "all the facts of the kerygmatic confession—incarnation, true manhood, death, resurrection, exaltation" (p. 79)—and even says that the kerygma is oriented "exclusively to the cross and resurrection, and especially to the incarnation of Jesus" (p. 81). Similarly, Erich Grässer, "Die politische Herausforderung an die biblische Theologie," *Evangelische Theologie*, 30 (1970): 232: "Therefore this kerygma can be called 'the Word' without a more precise definition, and this distinguishes it from all human words 'because it proclaims the glory of Christ that creates life and effects judgment' (Adolf Schlatter)." For criticism of Bultmann's concept of kerygma see Hans Albert, *Traktat über kritische Vernunft* (2d ed.; Tübingen: J. C. B. Mohr [Paul Siebeck], 1969), p. 114: "In [Bultmann's] case the limit of demythologizing has been drawn completely arbitrarily, indeed, by a thoroughly dogmatic point of view, namely, to retain as kerygma what he regards as the kernel of Christian faith—the kerygma."

cisely what Bultmann learned from dialectical theology, the basic relation to life, and thus it is more resistant to transformation and not even interested in working to improve the underlying situation. In any case, when Bultmann distinguished between kerygma and theology in the essay of 1929, "Church and Teaching in the New Testament,"[9] he did it in the interest of the criticism to which theology, as the discussion of doctrine, is subject; the kerygma, however, as address, claim, or—as I would interpret it with a non-Bultmannian expression—the "absolute" in Christian faith, is not subject to criticism. The liberation that love engenders and the claim that it lays upon us are absolutely binding; they are kerygmatic address, which, as Bultmann interprets Paul, "accosts each individual, throwing the person himself into question by rendering his self-understanding problematic, and demanding a decision of him."[10] The kerygma can be defined as "absolute" in two respects. First, it is unsurpassable, for no one can promise, give, or demand more than love; second, it is underivable, for it cannot be grounded within the world. Anthropology, especially psychology, can certainly provide hints that man is dependent upon love, but even these hints can be relativized by cultural anthropology; it cannot be established scientifically why the manipulation of man by man, or why cynical hatred, should not be better than love. The absolute calls for a decision that can be made rationally and is therefore intelligible, but which nonetheless is undemonstrable and therefore has a decisionist character. Thus, in Bultmann's

9. In *Faith and Understanding,* 1: 184–219.
10. Rudolf Bultmann, *Theology of the New Testament,* trans. Kendrick Grobel (New York: Scribner's, 1951), 1: 307.

case, the concept of kerygma includes a moment of decision, which is justified theologically if the contents of the
proclamation remain situational and are understood "historically." If, on the other hand, we understand kerygma as
traditional formulations of Christology or objectifications of
a doctrine, the legitimate moment of decision gives rise to
a total decisionism that identifies kerygma and theology,
withdrawing both from rational control.

Against this attempt to exempt, in principle, certain theological statements from criticism, Bultmann defends himself
in an early exchange with Karl Barth, who argued the thesis
"that the *pneuma Christou* cannot be regarded as compet-
ing with other spirits." Consistent with his later understanding of kerygma, Bultmann answers, "Yes and no!" Yes,
because the kerygma has absolute authority for the believer,
and appropriately is beyond competition. No, because "even
the witness of faith appears as a literary phenomenon,
standing as such alongside other expressions as a particular
point of view," which means that it is subject to criticism
and comparison.[11]

The difficulty with the concept of kerygma stems from an
inherent ambiguity, for the term can refer both to the act of
proclaiming and to the content of proclamation, to address
and to the imparting of information. If we focus on the act
itself, decision is necessary; but if the content—the "what"
of proclamation—is under discussion, then the kerygmatic
formulation must be subjected to criticism. Ebeling draws
a distinction between those formulations which are handed
down in precisely worded statements (which he calls "sus-

11. *Karl Barth–Rudolf Bultmann: Briefwechsel, 1922–1966*, ed. B.
Jaspert (Zürich: Theologischer Verlag, 1971), p. 11.

pended kerygma"), and "kerygma in the proper sense of an
address made here and now."[12] The fixed formulae in which
the kerygma is passed down always include "specific theological interpretations,"[13] and because of that, in the sense
of Bultmann's fundamental distinction between kerygma
and theology, a distinction to which Ebeling adheres, they
are subject to criticism. However, the passing down of such
kerygmatic formulae in no way guarantees that the act of
proclamation itself is passed on; indeed, quite the contrary.
Ebeling feels compelled to maintain the distinction between
kerygma that has been preserved in tradition and kerygma
that is actual event, and he introduces the concept of "situation" in which "kerygma can be understood as kerygma."[14]
The situation ought to be transformed from its mere given-
ness into a specific situation where the necessity of the
kerygma becomes evident. With this observation, Ebeling
comes very close to a political theology, but does not quite
reach it. The conceptual system that he has inherited and
employed is intra-theological and is not capable of actually
converting the "factual" situation of alienation—in which
men are not yet fully conscious of their suffering, since such
suffering is concealed with the help of industrial manipulation—into a "specific" situation that brings to light man's
essential need for liberation. The link between the two has
to be the burden of suffering brought about by social
conditions.

   For Bultmann the distinction between kerygma and theology remains intact, because, in essence, obedience is asso-

12. Ebeling, *Theology and Proclamation,* pp. 46, 45. See also his discussion of H. Schlier, pp. 120 ff.
13. Barth and Bultmann, *Briefwechsel,* p. 11.
14. Ebeling, *Theology and Proclamation,* pp. 53–54.

ciated with kerygma and criticism with theology. Particular theological contents must be examined again and again, so that the kerygma, which is itself beyond criticism, can appear in them.

> The kerygma, however, is always expressed in the conceptuality of human intercourse. Therefore, although kerygma and theology are fundamentally different, they are not separable in practice. That means that the exact content of the kerygma, how many and what affirmations it must contain, can never be definitely stated.[15]

The kerygma functions as a limiting concept and not as a material concept; it cannot be neatly summarized in a collection of propositional truths. Just as love, in various situations that are mutually exclusive, takes on unexpected but by no means arbitrary forms—for example, the political form of nonviolence, but, *ultima ratione*, also the form of counterviolence—the kerygma necessarily has various situational or relational theological forms. That means, however, that every form of kerygma—and we have this treasure only in earthen vessels, which can be broken but also created anew—must be subject to criticism. A theology that understands itself in this way (not a "theology of kerygma," for this expression is in fact a camouflage) would not betray the ideas of the Enlightenment and would pose no problem for the principles of historical-critical thought.

THE RENUNCIATION OF THE HISTORICAL JESUS

But what keeps theology from supplanting the kerygma by reducing it to doctrinal propositions? Both from a systematic perspective and from an understanding of church

15. Bultmann, *Faith and Understanding*, 1: 218.

history the answer is clear: the earthly, historical Jesus of
Nazareth. It is precisely within the perplexities of this problem that the heritage of dialectical theology proves fatal,
for under its influence Bultmann has sharply formulated his
rejection of the historical Jesus as a rejection of liberalism.

Perhaps the vain and unsuccessful attempt of liberal
theology to produce a biography of Jesus and to accommodate him to our situation with the help of this portrait,
played a part in Bultmann's criticism of the liberal position.
Surely it cannot be understood as a simple dogmatic rejection of the relevance of the historical Jesus. Bultmann,
responding to the "new quest for the historical Jesus," has
explicitly agreed with Braun and likewise with Käsemann
"that the earthly Jesus is the criterion of the kerygma and
its legitimation."[16] That certainly does not mean that the
historical Jesus in effect "supersedes" the biblical Christ.[17]
It seems to me that the real point of contention within the
Bultmannian school is rooted in this tension between the
kerygma and the historical Jesus. Do we begin with the
kerygmatic Christ and use the historical Jesus as a corrective
with which to evaluate the message (qua Bultmann)? Or
do we focus primarily on the historical Jesus himself (qua
Braun) and understand the kerygma as the absoluteness of
his claim—not thereby as an additional content that makes
faith possible in the first place, but as the form in which
Jesus encounters us today? If we ask in appropriate fashion
where Bultmann grounds his renunciation of the historical

16. Bultmann, *Glauben und Verstehen*, 4 vols. (Tübingen: J. C. B.
Mohr [Paul Siebeck], 1933–65), 4: 169.
17. Schmithals, "Noch einmal: Historischer und biblischer Jesus,"
Evangelische Kommentare, 3 (1970): 417.

Jesus (or, e.g., what Schmithals's objection is to the historical Jesus), then the critical points are reduced to two: first,
Jesus as an historical figure is subject to historical relativism,
which means he is not unique. Therefore, in the second
place "only the law" is expressed in his message, while the
proclamation of him brings the gospel for the first time.

The Relativity of Jesus

With regard to the first argument, that "everything
historical inherently bears the character of relativity and
is, therefore, interchangeable with other historical dimensions,"[18] it seems to me that one is not compelled to draw
the conclusion that Jesus is rendered interchangeable or
indeed superfluous. The fact that what Jesus essentially was
continues under other names and in other figures detracts
nothing from his unsubstitutable particularity but rather is
a necessary part of it. But regardless of how one judges the
interchangeability or uniqueness of historical men, it appears to me that the kerygmatic *salto mortale*—which says
that we must reject the historical Jesus because only the
biblical Christ guarantees a dogmatically assured uniqueness—cannot withstand a serious verification of truth. From
the book by Hans Albert, the critical rationalist and student
of Popper, who devotes a chapter to the Bultmannian theology, I have methodically drawn the conclusion that such
procedures do not withstand the probing of critical reason,
because "critical thinking . . . is suspended, purely arbitrarily, precisely at the point" where one can no longer
make use of it since it leads to unacceptable consequences.

---

18. Schmithals, "Kein Streit um des Kaisers Bart," p. 78.

"All things considered, these representatives manage to
make their theology both critical and dogmatic: critical in
the things that are relatively unimportant, dogmatic in those
that appear more important."[19] Even if one does not share
the neopositivistic perspective and its understanding of
"critical reason" that underlies this critique, it remains a
must to acknowledge and assume the canons of scholarly
ethics as represented and reflected by Albert, and to do
so, moreover, with highest regard for the veracity of the
critical results brought to a conclusion by Albert Schweitzer.
One can perhaps understand and interpret dogmas such
as the uniqueness of Jesus, but the method of thought cannot
be partly dogmatic and partly critical, for enlightenment
is indivisible.

If we can attain or preserve the uniqueness of Jesus only
by wrenching him out of history or by having to appeal to a
mere abstraction of that history (e.g., to the sheer "*that* of
his appearance"), then the price is too high. The theological
task consists not in the suspension of a probing, comparative
reason for the sake of faith, but only in our recognition of
the meaning of Jesus within history and its relativities. Only
the relative Jesus can motivate us to act, only with him can
we become contemporary, only because he is a figure in
history comparable with other dimensions and with us can
we enter into a non-authoritarian relationship with him that
is capable of transforming us. The "authoritative lordship"
of the gospel remains an empty claim; the historical-relative
Jesus, on the other hand, give us the possibility that we have
with respect to all historical figures, namely, of learning

19. Hans Albert, *Trakat über kritische Vernunft* (2d ed., Tübingen:
J. C. B. Mohr [Paul Siebeck], 1969), pp. 110, 129.

from them, and that means more than being subject to them
or obeying them.

The "Legitimation" of the Message

The second problem that the historical Jesus poses for
kerygmatic theology is that of legitimation. Such theology
is of the opinion that we can hear only the law from Jesus'
own message; only the kerygma about Jesus bears promise
as gospel. Whether this reproach applies to Bultmann is
highly questionable. His understanding of indicative and
imperative surely does not depend upon the distinction
between the kerygmatic and the historical Jesus. It is not
the exacting demand, which is found throughout the New
Testament, that characterizes the law as *mortificatio*. Nor is
every concrete deliberation of action within society abolished because it has reference to law. Rather the *vivificatio*
of the gospel lies precisely in its encouragement or liberation for action. Whether, for example, the injunction, "Go
and do likewise!" is understood as law or as gospel depends
upon its results: does it enslave men by imposing additional
restraints, or does it speak to them of their own powerlessness and self-made corruption? The undialectical usage of
the formula "law and gospel" (and this usage is typical
today, from the Confessing Movement and church leader-
ship to neoorthodoxy) is oriented not toward what law and
gospel do, *facere (vivificatio* and *mortificatio)*, but instead
remains purely formal, while statements that denote completed action (it is fulfilled, Christ has set us free, the Cru-
cified One gives understanding) are played off against
imperative statements. Bultmann, in spite of all this, has
dealt rather precisely with the difference between act and

work, between a free act of obedience and self-justification
by man's own achievement; and the trivial contention that
every reflection made by sociopolitical theology would be
"law" can hardly appeal to him. Such a contention belongs
to a whole network of false alternatives that bias the entire
critique of political theology by kerygmatic neoorthodoxy.
In addition to law and gospel, I can mention the alternatives of structure and person (Thielicke), of exegesis and
sociology, of social and eschatological events. All these
apparent alternatives, which are usually linked with the "not
. . . but . . ." formula, derive from a God-world dualism,
for which no firm basis is to be found in the historical Jesus.
Such dualism leads to an understanding of revelation as
otherworldly and supernatural, which within the Christian
tradition has been criticized again and again by appeal to
the historical Jesus and the Old Testament. That the ves-
tiges of this controversy regarding a worldly—and that
always means political—understanding of salvation versus
a dualistic, unworldly understanding reach even into the
Gospel of John has been demonstrated by Luise Schottroff
in an essay on Jesus' encounter with the Samaritan woman
at the well.[20] The danger persists that this theologically
necessary dialogue, which is found in the New Testament
itself, will be extinguished within the Bultmannian School
by its exclusive concentration on the doctrinal content of
the kerygma, an outcome that would have definite political
and ecclesio-political consequences.

20. Luise Schottroff, "Joh. 4:5–15 und die Konsequenzen des johan-
neischen Dualismus," *Zeitschrift für die neutestamentliche Wissen-
schaft und die Kunde des Urchristentums*, 60 (1969): 194–214.

THE DEPOLITICIZING OF THE GOSPEL

This concentration on the kerygma—as a necessary formal principle—validates or dogmatizes its material contents in the form of new doctrinal propositions; this leads to an indifferent ideological superstructure that remains independent of the situation and indistinguishable in function from undemythologized theology. The more abstract the theological concepts it employs—such as redemption, sin, grace, resurrection—the more kerygmatically pure and less worldly it will conceive itself to be and the further it will retreat from the worldliness of Jesus as portrayed in his words and deeds. This is not at all a problem of a different level of language, in which case scholarship would naturally have to plead for a higher level of abstraction, but the problem of extraordinarily diverse dynamics of language. It appears to me that a deductive theology which begins with kerygma in fixed propositional forms has much less chance of being understood. The inductive theological method demanded today is not simply a response to some fashionable whim; it accords rather with a growing awareness of the significance of comparative, critical investigation, which Protestant theology had already accepted in historical criticism but lost again through the reaction of dialectical theology. This comparative method that challenges its own opinions accords not only with the "children of a scientific generation" (Brecht), but even more with the language of Jesus. The abandonment of Jesus' language because the kerygma appears in it only indirectly and "impurely" signifies in effect a depoliticizing of the gospel, which, like every intended depoliticizing, is only apparent, since by remaining silent it effectively sanctions existing conditions and the politics of prevailing structures. It is a dangerous presumption to suppose that theological propositions are to be understood chiefly as "purely" theological, having no political presuppositions, content, or consequences. Such a conception encourages the dualistic bifurcation of reality into two hierarchically arranged realms—faith above, politics below. Similarly, it overlooks the fact that even in seemingly apolitical statements and concepts certain politically desirable attitudes are honored and utilized. Humility, modesty, exercise of one's own will, and subordination are examples of religious virtues that are deduced from "purely" theological judgments. For example, if redemption is understood as the capacity of man for a "new obedience"—and this is how it is presented in most theological handbooks, dictionaries, and textbooks—then the emancipatory-biblical motif, which understands redemption essentially as "liberation," fades into the background.

The tendency found in historical criticism toward emancipation from untested assumptions and uncontrolled authority is subsequently formalized and theologically obliterated. Criticism is reduced to a mere technical medium, which encourages impartiality toward the texts but not toward their political content. The less worldly and the more "purely" theologically it is conceived, the better theology functions as a medium of social accommodation. An unworldly conception of obedience clears the way for this accommodation, which takes place on a level where the degree of abstraction is below that of theology—especially in books on religious education. Some examples drawn from religious education texts currently in use will serve as illustrations. The real problems—for example, the problem of man's alienation from labor—are glossed over:

> Christian existence is . . . a calling that is dependent not so much on talent and disposition as on obedience to God, and is determined not by what we deserve but by how we serve. With this undertanding of calling even an undesirable calling has significance.[21]

War is classified under "God's punishments, trials, afflictions, like pestilence and famine." As the Christian knows, war is "ultimately decided not in the general headquarters of the armies, but in the hand of God."[22] In this instance, obedience and trust in God serve to encourage fatalism and to discredit efforts to bring about peace. As in the case of obedience, concepts like justice and love are also apparently depoliticized, but in reality they are adapted precisely to sanction the status quo. "The message of the Bible does not abolish social distinctions, but does rid them of malice. Its solution does not mean equality, but justice and love."[23]

The political import of such statements is the stabilization of the class structure. To be sure, the blame cannot be laid directly to dialectical theology; but it is obvious just

21. *Vom Glauben eines Christen*, vol. 9 of *Wort und Zeugnis*, ed. Herborner Kreis (Frankfurt: Moritz Diesterweg, 1965), p. 45.

22. *Lehrbuch für evangelische Unterweisung*, Part III of *Am Quell des Lebens*, ed. P. Börger (6th ed.; Heidelberg: Quelle & Meyer, 1960), p. 284.

23. W. Pfendsack, *Kennst du den Weg? Eine christliche Unterweisung* (6th ed.; Basel: F. Reinhardt, n.d.). In the meantime, this book has been published in a revised form that alters this quotation entirely in the sense of the criticism intended here. "Social distinctions are not directly abolished in the Bible (for example, the master-slave relationship in Eph. 6:3–9). Still, in its call to justice and love lies a revolutionary transforming power, which cannot be resigned to existing relations but must rather struggle to overcome them" (1971 ed., p. 81).

how little dialectical theology and existentialist interpretation, especially with their latter-day curtailment of the
kerygma, offer criteria by which these theologically "pure,"
unpolitical statements can be criticized and their eminent
political import comprehended. The fact that social interests find expression in theological formulations remains
concealed, and its positive implications are not explored.
Only the highest degree of consciousness, the complete
identification with the interests of the poor, could abolish
this ideological illusion of a purely apolitical speech and
become "impure," combining the political and the theological as in the language of Jesus. Jesus' call for salvation for
the poor (Luke 6:20) and his partiality against the rich
(Matt. 19:24) stem from an obvious political consciousness.
For him salvation could not be compartmentalized, and no
sphere of life was excluded. Accordingly, his language was
"impure," and that means it could not be reckoned according to spheres of existence, nor was it based on a so-called
proprium of faith. Rather it was ambiguous in its possibilities of application and for that reason controversial; it was
unequivocal only in its concern for liberation. In distinction
to theological language, which has supposedy been depoliticized but thereby in fact has become subservient to
the prevailing interests, the language of Jesus is always both
religious and political, encountering the whole man in his
social environment.

Adherence to the language of Jesus would enjoin us to
rediscover the political relevance of the gospel. The renunciation of the historical Jesus and the substitution of kerygmatic formulae for his language serve to enhance the
depoliticizing of the gospel. From the perspective of church

politics such renunciation can have only the effect of silenc-
ing criticism directed against the church. Thus, it is with
good reason that Schmithals writes: "The church has never
been interested in the what and how of Jesus' life."[24]

Only the victor could make such a statement and it is
from this point of view that the religious education texts
customarily portray church history. Sacrifice cannot find its
place in such an understanding of the church. The hierarchies of the large churches could not have been interested
in the what and how of Jesus' life, because this interest
would have called them radically into question (for example, in regard to money, oaths, military service). Christians
from Peter Waldo and Michael Servetus to Henri Perrin or
Don Mazzi, who were interested in the message of the
gospel, have been persecuted and punished for these interests. The official church uses the kerygmatic Christ as a
suitable means of discipline. It was the biblical Christ,
whom we seek to recognize today as the historical Jesus,
who bothered the Grand Inquisitor and even the petty
Protestant inquisitors. In other words, the Christ who rules
in the church and who has supplanted the biblical Christ
is the Christ of the rulers.

The answer to the question concerning the role of dialectical theology within the Bultmannian synthesis and its
significance for a possible political theology can be summarized as follows: The authority of the text is its historical
claim in a particular situation. When kerygma is understood
as absolute claim—by contrast with its dogmatic objectifications—it demands a worldly and therefore, in theory at

24. Schmithals, "Kein Streit um des Kaisers Bart," p. 81.

least, a political interpretation of the gospel. Recourse to
the historical Jesus, who is perceived as a corrective to the
dogmatic Christ, is thereby necessary; renunciation of the
historical Jesus would also be renunciation of the political
Jesus.

*Diagram of the Origin and Further
Development of Bultmannian Theology*

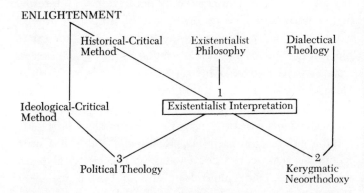

Bultmann's synthesis in the form of existentialist interpretation (1) is based on historical-critical method, existentialist philosophy, and dialectical theology. But shortly after
Bultmann the contradictory elements stand out more sharply,
and two possible developments are discernible. Kerygmatic
neoorthodoxy (2) clings obstinately to what Bultmann has
taken from dialectical theology, but without bringing it
into a productive relation with historical criticism. Historical criticism and the dogmatics of kerygma fall apart, while
the third pillar of the synthesis, existentialist reflection,
which for Bultmann himself was able to mediate between

the other two, crumbles away. An alternative to this development lies in a conversation with the ideological-critical method, which also stems from the Enlightenment and is consistent with historical-critical thinking. With its help existentialist interpretation is developed further into political theology (3).

4. Existentialist Philosophy

The significance of existentialist philosophy for Bultmann's thought will be examined here by focusing on two concepts, the understanding of existence and the understanding of history. In the course of this discussion greater attention must be directed to the political critique of both concepts.

Bultmann's synthesis between the claim of absoluteness, as expressed by the alien and nonderivable message of dialectical theology, and historical criticism, which relativizes all alleged revelation, would not have been possible without a philosophical framework that aimed at overcoming historical relativism, but without reviving the old metaphysical positions.

THE UNDERSTANDING OF EXISTENCE

Why did the concept of existence developed by Heidegger in the twenties prove relevant for Bultmann? Because Heidegger conceived existence essentially as historical existence. For Bultmann the self-understanding of man goes further astray, "the more it flees from its own history."[1] It finds itself in the understanding of its radical historicity,

1. Rudolf Bultmann, *History and Eschatology: The Presence of Eternity* (New York: Harper Torchbook, 1962), p. 149.

that is, in the way it is related to the future—not the future
as made or projected but the future received as that which
arrives (*Zukünftigkeit*). The man who continually renews
his self-understanding through this possibility that comes
to him does not need, even in a spiritual sense, to cling to
what is past or present, or to what he possesses. He becomes
free from himself, and that means "being open for the
future, not seizing it, but surrendering himself as it were to
the future"; it means "being open for what the moment
offers me at any time."[2] But can this openness to which the
gospel frees us be conceived apolitically, in a vacuum of
crucial life-possibilities and fortunes? From a theoretical
point of view, existentialist philosophy as Bultmann understands it offers no basis for an apolitical interpretation, but
Bultmann *de facto* limits this openness to individualistic
existence. For example, he summarizes Rom. 14:17 as follows: "The reign of God . . . is righteousness and peace and
joy in the Holy Spirit." He then proceeds to interpret: "And
that means: the conception of bliss is thought of with regard to the individual."[3] This is to be inferred not from the
Pauline context but no doubt from the nineteenth-century
bourgeoisie. The charge raised here by political theology,
especially by Johannes Metz, against existentialist interpretation proceeds on the assumption that salvation has been
reduced to privatistic categories; in other words, it has been
reduced to a matter that affects only the individual as an
individual.

Regarding this point, the objection is raised by those on
the right that forgiveness of sins—the very basis of salva-

2. Rudolf Bultmann, *Glauben und Verstehen,* 4 vols. (Tübingen:
J. C. B. Mohr [Paul Siebeck] 1933–65), 3:210.
3. Bultmann, *History and Eschatology,* p. 42.

tion—necessarily concerns the individual. Not only the understanding of man as sinner but also the reception of salvation should be based on the ego; and the significance of individual life disclosed in this understanding could never again be nullified without surrendering the thing itself, namely, the understanding of man as justified sinner. This conflict, however, between those who insist upon the immeasurable significance of the individual and those who emphasize the collective in contrast to the individual is unfruitful, because a proper understanding of existence, even of individual existence, is inconceivable apart from a social context. Even our personal decisions are determined by social behavior patterns that bear the stamp of the classes to which we belong. Regarding collective sins and liabilities, the tendency toward pure individualism has virtually disappeared: even the individual Pole whose family was murdered by my countrymen can forgive me, an individual German, only if my country accepts the boundaries of a new peace, only if fear is calmed by political action. The political situation, to be sure, does not constitute the forgiveness of sins, for that depends entirely on the other person; but it is an unalterable prerequisite, and without it neither the Pole nor perhaps even God, who certainly does not stage this behind the Pole's back, can or will forgive me. Here we must be very concrete in our discussion if we are to get to the root of the problem. Some people object that forgiveness is decidedly not a question of such formidable and concrete matters as those between Poles and Germans, but of God's eschatological forgiveness of the individual's original sin. But this objection only exposes its proponents,[4]

4. For discussion, cf. Erich Grässer, "Die politische Herausforderung an die biblische Theologie," *Evangelische Theologie,* 30 (1970): 237.

insofar as sin and forgiveness are both taken out of history and abstractly individualized.

It appears to me that such individualistic curtailments and ontological generalizations do not necessarily follow from the basic assumptions regarding the historicity of existence and the futurity of salvation. With Bultmann the understanding of existence has been formalized even more highly than with Heidegger—which means, however, that the concrete particulars of these formal principles, which are rooted in the cultural-critical mood of the twenties, are capable of revision. For instance, it is not necessary to belabor the way in which Bultmann defames concepts like program, theory, principle, organization.[5] On this matter he thinks in a bourgeois and presociological fashion: in other words, an essential presupposition of modern political theory is omitted in his work—namely, the distinction between state and society, a distinction which in fact is constitutive of every political theology. The categories with which he treats the relation to the state (compared to which society has no rights of its own) accord perfectly with Lutheran doctrine, for there are only two: obedience or—in extreme cases—martyrdom. There can be no place in this pre-democratic way of thinking for participation in decision making, constructive criticism, and political change, not to mention revolutionary transformation of existing structures. This model is applied in a similar way to other authorities, for example, the family, university, and church. The modes of behavior sanctioned by this model are either submission or departure, subordination or emi-

5. Cf., e.g., Bultmann, *Glauben und Verstehen*, 2: 14 and 16.

gration. A constructive posture that resolves the contradictions present in actual institutions and thereby changes the institution is inconceivable in this context. Only the individual can be changed, not the structures. These notions have indeed found support in existentialist philosophy and its preoccupation with subjectivity, but they are not necessarily characteristic of it.

Even more important is another omission particularly evident in the punctiliar character of this understanding of existence. Bultmann is certainly aware that man is determined by his past—and what else should that mean except that he is subject to biological, social, and psychological forces, and therefore does not have freedom at his disposal but urgently needs liberation from time to time? However, this is a formal insight which remains unpacked. Existentialist interpretation neglects the conditions of its own preunderstanding. It grounds itself in the experience of the eschatological moment, which transcends all conditions. In its fascination with this unworldly moment, existentialist interpretation fails to consider the stamp left upon man by his past, by his origin and place; thus it overlooks the bondage arising from the fact that we come from a definite history, even though, theoretically, it retains this concrete type of bondage in its notion of the historicity of existence. It is not surprising that this real historicity is nonexistent for those students of Bultmann who believe they can replace existentialist reflection by kerygmatic repetition. Metz concurs with this critique: "If we want to deal with existence we cannot today speak purely existentially."[6] Käsemann

6. Johannes Metz, *Theology of the World,* trans. William Glen-Doepel (New York: Herder & Herder, 1969), p. 127.

also, in opposition to Bultmann, speaks of our "utter entanglement with the world," not only for the man prior to
faith, but even for the man in faith.[7] If, on the other hand,
deprivatization of proclamation is called for, it does not
mean a depersonalization in which the person, his opinions,
his anxieties, and expectations would no longer be present.
On the contrary, being a person first becomes a concrete,
tangible reality precisely when one becomes aware of his
dependence on society and, conjointly, of the latitude permitted by that society at specific points. Any attempt to
keep Christian proclamation free from this mutual relation
between man and his society leads—certainly not to heresy,
for that risk is left only to those Christians who unite religious and social existence—but to a boredom inherent to
faith and the elite congregation, to theological *l'art-pour-
l'art*, to the so-called totally pure *proprium* of faith, which
is represented partly by highly specialized theological jargon and partly by the language of the sixteenth century,
which for us serves devotional purposes.[8] In short, it leads
to pure ideology, because it is ideology without foundation
and without praxis.

THE UNDERSTANDING OF HISTORY

If we ask how such appearances of mummification could
arise in existentialist theology, then we must analyze Bultmann's understanding of history, which was produced in

7. Ernst Käsemann, "Von theologischen Recht historisch–kritischer
Exegese," *Zeitschrift für Theologie und Kirche*, 64 (1967): 276.
8. Cf., for example, the opinion of the Theological Commission of the
EKU: *Zum Verständnis des Todes Jesu*, ed. F. Viering (Gütersloh:
Gütersloher Verlagshaus G. Mohn, 1968). For a critical response see
Dorothee Soelle, "Zum Dialog zwischen Theologie und Literaturwis-
senschaft," *Internationale Dialogzeitschrift*, 2 (1969): 299 ff.

essence by opposing and circumscribing the Greek understanding of history. Bultmann's real contribution lies in his
clear distinction between the conceptions of history found
in Greek thought and in the Old Testament. The Greeks, on
the one hand, held to a naturalistic understanding of history
marked by the image of a recurring cycle governed by prescribed laws, in which God remained transcendent vis-à-vis
the individual and the process of coming to be and passing
away. The understanding of history developed by the Old
Testament, on the other hand, takes note of the categories
of decision, human responsibility, and man's elemental relation to the future. The historical understanding of human
existence—in which existence is determined by the historical situation and the decisions that interrupt it, and not by
some unalterable substance or preprogrammed character—
coheres naturally with the Old Testament view and predis-
poses the Bultmannian position toward a political and
social understanding of human life, within which eschatological decisions pertain to neither the inner man, nor
another world, nor life after death. Within the Jewish
understanding of history, acting, making decisions, responding to situations, and creating situations are not accidents
that have no effect upon the unalterable person of the one
doing the acting; rather, it is precisely in those activities
that man reforms himself, is converted to God, or worships
other gods. Within this perspective, however, although not
formulated in this way by Bultmann, the world is conceived
as transformable. Not only must the ordinances established
from the beginning be preserved and defended—as in
Lutheranism's understanding of the world—but these ordinances can themselves be transformed. Their validity can

be called into question at any time in accord with the various needs of men.

The question is: How far has Bultmann himself carried out this progressive tendency? Has he not been influenced more strongly by the sense of being at the mercy of history and by the threat of history?[9] Metz sees in this the danger that the history of the beginning has more and more supplanted the history of the end, and although this is inconsistent with Bultmann's anti-Greek interest in the future, it does, *de facto*, determine his understanding, especially in *History and Eschatology*. There the problem is posed by the abandonment of the question of meaning in history, that is, the reduction of the question of meaning to individual existence.[10] Bultmann reports this reduction chiefly as an historian discussing various philosophies of history, but then—with a certain congeniality toward Jacob Burckhardt —has adopted it. By virtue of this individualistic constriction, Bultmann is not in a position to demythologize or to interpret New Testament cosmology; he must eliminate it, whereas a political theology can read the political intentions inherent in these cosmological images. The final result of this way of thinking about Christian faith and history is summarized in the statement: "The meaning of history always lies in the present." The man who cannot perceive this meaning is advised to turn his back on universal history and to look at his own personal history, to discern there the meaningfulness of his own responsible decisions.[11] This con-

9. Cf. Bultmann, *History and Eschatology*, pp. 2, 10–11, 43 and passim.
10. Ibid., pp. 74 ff.
11. Ibid., p. 155.

ception, of course, enters upon a field to which the critical method is no longer applicable. In the face of such a statement, we have no right to disregard the interests that produced it, which means concretely that we must raise the questions originally posed by Karl Marx. Whose interest is served by perceiving the meaning of history always in the present? To which class do those persons belong who talk that way? By what expectations are they determined and by what achievements? Can people who are honeycombed in the Brazilian ghettos talk like that? Does this statement not presuppose that one has been saturated with certain bourgeois ideals? Can we repeat it today, in view of the fact that two-thirds of all men—from the beginnings of their life and without "responsible decision"—belong to the wretched of the earth?

With this statement Bultmann avoids the presumption of claiming to know the end of world history. As a critical statement against a biblicistic interpretation of apocalyptic, which perpetuates and reifies the late-Hellenistic expectation of the end of the world, this kind of reduction is legitimate and proper. But does this debate with a stale Christian ideology represent, on the whole, a serious level of discussion? We must ask whether Bultmann has not let his way of asking the question be dictated by unusually provincial ecclesiastical thoughts, and of exclusively German origin. Has he not limited his debate to clerical opponents who are not attentive to the real problems—just as those concerning the wretched of the earth—because they approach them with antiquated answers?

Why has the concern for demythologizing, if it is after all a part of the enlightened movement, gnawed away ex-

clusively at mythology? Who made the prior decision that
mythology would be our essential and sole problem? We
can no longer claim that the Christian tradition has posed
this problem for us; on the contrary, it is merely a narrow
provincial channel within the broad stream of Christianity.
Theology's partner in this conversation remains the church,
not the world. Many non-Christians consider the demythologizing debate a mere defense mechanism, because theology, which understands itself as a critical enterprise,
is dodging the decisive reproach of the Enlightenment,
namely, that of sanctioning irrational structures of power
and authority and of hindering the liberation of man by the
obstruction of enlightenment. The reproach against religion
as lodged by the Enlightenment and by the Marxists runs
as follows: Christians, especially theologians, are "deceived
deceivers"—deceived by the mythological-dogmatic thinking
forced upon them institutionally, deceivers because they
employ unconscious or perhaps half-conscious deception to
sanction existing law and order. Demythologizing has been
able to refute only the first charge; and if it does not go
further and develop a political interpretation of the gospel,
it has merely created an area free of conflict or, as Käsemann says, "an indispensable, though by no means exclusive, mode of interpretation."[12]

INTERPRETATIONS OF HOPE

Bultmann's seclusion from world-historical, political, social thought has been strengthened by his appropriation of
existentialist philosophy, a fact seen most clearly when we

12. Ernst Käsemann, *Jesus Means Freedom*, trans. Frank Clarke
(Philadelphia: Fortress, 1970), p. 132. (Translation altered.)

bear in mind the deficient understanding of hope in existentialist interpretation. Bultmann distinguishes three biblical
forms of hope: first, the prophetic, in which the hope that
God will intervene and establish justice is contingent upon
the condition that the people fulfill their obligation of
obedience; second, the apocalyptic hope in which the end
comes—independently of man—at a time prescribed by
God; and finally, the Christian-eschatological hope, especially as it is found in the Gospel of John, in which history
is swallowed up by realized eschatology and innerworldly
hope becomes superfluous. Bultmann's criticism of the
mythological-apocalyptic hope is justified in the sense that
it is an historical criticism of mythical representations of
the world. It is also a legitimate criticism of the confused
blending of these forms of hope by Moltmann whose "theology of hope" becomes, *de facto*, a mythology of apocalyptic
promise. However, the reduction of Christian faith to the
eschatological certainty of salvation experienced in fleeting
moments binds Bultmann more closely than he perhaps
wishes to the hopelessness that results from historicism.
Bultmann succeeds in delimiting Dilthey's "eschatology
transformed into aestheticism," or Croce's view that "every
present moment is an eschatological moment,"[13] and in
really overcoming historicism, only in respect to the individual's relation to the coming future. Bultmann's future is
indeed "open" to the extent that the "genuine life"[14] of the
individual can be gained or lost, but it is not open for the
peace that has meaning for all people. That, however,
makes it difficult to explain why early Christianity was so

13. Bultmann, *History and Eschatology*, pp. 125, 135–136.
14. Ibid., p. 142.

quick to exchange its eschatological hope for a material-sacramental present. Why, in other words, did the eschatological community become the cult of early catholicism? It seems evident to me that this development was accelerated because both forms of hope that play a significant role in Bultmann's work—not only the self-sufficient, unworldly hope of the present, but also the apocalyptic-mythological, which reduces men and their actions to mere pawns in the divine chess game—forgot their Jewish origins in prophetic hope. Mythology and withdrawal from the world are only two sides of the same coin of hopelessness. Such hopelessness expects nothing more from man, and it triumphs today in the form of Lutheran orthodoxy, which is not yet rid of that disdain for humanity characteristic of late antiquity and the late Middle Ages, a disdain that sees itself as devotion to God.[15]

Bultmann discusses the problem of hope only in terms of the conflicts between apocalyptic mythology and the eschatological present; the first Jewish form of hope, to which every political theology is necessarily tied, namely, prophecy, has been omitted. The sharpest criticism of Bultmann at this point stems from the Jewish philosopher Ernst Bloch, who sets forth another understanding of myth. Bloch interrogates every myth as to its tendency and inquires after the intentions of mythical language, while Bultmann is concerned about the objectifying images of myth. Bultmann demythologizes what the myth says and what mythology implies by way of spatial and temporal representations. Bloch asks what the myth is aiming at, and dis-

15. Cf. H. Blumenberg, *Die Legitimität der Neuzeit* (Frankfurt: Suhrkamp Verlag, 1966), pp. 433 ff.

covers the "rebellious-eschatological myth" as a form of slave-language for men who cannot openly express their hopes. Bloch refers not to the "transcendent-hypostasizing" myths of Bultmann but to the "transcending, Utopian-forming" myths of the subversive human spirit.[16]

The abandonment of the question regarding the meaning of history in the case of Bultmann has its exegetical pendant in the abandonment of the Jewish-prophetic forms of hope and in the suppression of the historical Jesus. Political theology, on the other hand, draws several conclusions from the Jewish-Christian dialogue, though not the conclusions drawn by dialectical theology, which relate primarily to the themes of election and salvation history. What we can learn today from Judaism has little to do with the reading off of a salvation history. I should like to list these points as follows: (1) criticism of Christian perfectionism, which despises man when it represents everyone as completed, finished, fulfilled, and redeemed; (2) a new understanding of man as *cooperator Dei* (not nourished by an artificially sustained antithesis to Catholicism), for which man is no longer seen as a passive agent receiving orders and grace; (3) a new understanding of repentance as real transformation and conversion. Formulated positively: faith is possible, love comes to pass, hope transforms men and their world.

16. Ernst Bloch, *Atheism in Christianity*, trans. J. T. Swan (New York: Herder & Herder, 1972), pp. 50–51.

5. Political Theology as Hermeneutic

We have tried to show that a political interpretation of the gospel is not antithetical to the essential intentions of Bultmann's theology. On the contrary, we have adopted several of its themes: the need for criticism (Chapter 2), the claim of absoluteness (Chapter 3), and the orientation toward personal self-understanding (Chapter 4).

But still lacking is a theology that has reflected systematically upon the relation of faith and politics. The history of the Constantinian era has bequeathed to us a heritage of suspicion and uncertainty regarding this relation. Because the church was intimately involved in politics, because it assumed the functions of shaping and maintaining the state and took its place among the powerful elite, often by abandoning or suppressing its own message, many Christians today plead for neutrality. From this shameful historical experience the conclusion is drawn that the church must remain neutral and transcend partisan politics; at most, the individual Christian can and should become involved in political activities. From this perspective a "political theology" is besieged by insurmountable problems. It is feared the gospel would disintegrate into socialist strategy and that

Christians would be reduced to "useful idiots," bent on undermining the liberal-democratic foundation of capitalistic societies. One is afraid of a new totalitarian certitude, for which politics is not based on rationality but is undergirded instead by an ideology that claims to have an insight into the whole of history—an ideology that conceives its values as ultimate and therefore proceeds in totalitarian fashion even in choosing the means by which to accomplish its objective. But "political theology" is not the same as a theologically grounded politics.

THE MEANING OF THE CONCEPT

For several reasons the phrase, "political interpretation of the gospel," which is comparable to such expressions as "existentialist" or "nonreligious" interpretation, appears to be a somewhat happier choice of terms than "political theology." In a discussion with J. B. Metz, Hans Maier has called attention to the burden imposed on the concept of "political theology" by its history, particularly as its meaning has been interpreted by Carl Schmitt.[1] According to Schmitt, the social structures of an epoch must cohere with its metaphysical view of the world if a genuine stability is to be guaranteed. Therefore, in 1922 Schmitt predicted the imminent demise of modern liberalism and democracy and their replacement by dictatorship, because the social and political structures of the former lacked theological foundation and elevation. In his view, which is nourished by Western history, political theology has essentially sanctioned

1. Hans Maier, " 'Politische Theologie'? Einwände eines Laien," in *Diskussion zur "politischen Theologie,"* ed. H. Peukert (Mainz/Munich: Chr. Kaiser/Grünewald, 1969), pp. 3, 4, 11.

and affirmed the existing order by "identifying the Christian promise with temporal-political forms," whereas today it is essentially a critical theology for which promises do not have an elevating function, but serve rather as standards by which the social structures must be judged. Thus Maier considers political theology, not without a certain historical justification, to be an "attempt at an unsuitable concept"; for ever since Augustine's classical critique, all forms "of theological transfiguration, especially of worldly powers and phenomena," are subject to the charge of idolatry, insofar as they transform politics into theology; in other words, the provisional and penultimate character of the political must be taken seriously.

The objection to the concept of political theology for historical reasons leads to the conclusion that the political theology of today would have to be the same as that of the Constantinian era; only the marks of identification would be reversed. This objection is encountered even in Protestant criticism, where it betrays a strange, vacuous way of thinking—the most formal instance imaginable of forcing agreement between two dissimilar realities in order to subsume under a collective category (such as totalitarianism), and thus *de facto* to equate things that in origin and intention are diametrically opposed to each other (such as national socialism and communism). For Maier, the only distinction between the older affirmative political theology and the more recent critical one lies "in the fact that the former's identification with the past and present is now transferred to the future"—as if these were arbitrarily interchangeable tenses and the qualitative distinction did not consist precisely in the reference either to what is given, what endures, what is at hand, or to the future. With regard to theological content it is a question of the "hierarchical ordering of faith and politics,"[2] an ordering based on the assumption that faith stands above politics, since it originates in God, while politics is derived solely from man. This assumption is coordinate with a dualism that plainly contradicts the proclamation of Jesus.

Another misunderstanding of the concept of political theology is closely associated with this hierarchical arrangement, namely, the opinion that political theology is merely "an auxiliary theological discipline concerned primarily with questions of politics or the social responsibility of the believer."[3] Such a theology of politics (yet another "theology of . . .") is not to be equated with political theology. Hence I prefer the expression "political interpretation" or "political hermeneutic." Accordingly, church attitudes toward political and social questions, political worship and activities, and concrete support for politically involved groups are limiting cases reflecting the concrete application of political theology. The concept itself must be conceived in broader terms.

When combined with theology, "political" does not mean that theology should now exchange its content for that of political science; precisely the same misjudgment was made a generation ago by those who attributed to existentialist theology an exchange of themes, asserting that it spoke only of man. Furthermore, political theology is not an attempt

2. E. Höflich, "Heilsverkündigung als politische Gewissensbildung, Eine Antwort auf Hans Maiers Polemik gegen die politische Theologie," *Frankfurter Hefte* (December, 1969), p. 851.
3. Ibid., p. 844.

to develop a concrete political program from faith, nor is it another type of Social Gospel in which praxis simply swallows up theory. There are no specifically Christian solutions to world problems for which a political theology would have to develop the theory. Political theology is rather a theological hermeneutic, which, in distinction from a theology that interprets reality from an ontological or existentialist point of view, holds open an horizon of interpretation in which politics is understood as the comprehensive and decisive sphere in which Chrstian truth should become praxis.

THE PREUNDERSTANDING OF POLITICAL THEOLOGY

But what is changed by this horizon of interpretation? We understand the gospel in its seriousness only when we consider the political horizon of life, only when we become aware that the failure or attainment of life is governed by social presuppositions and belongs to the political dimension of existence. The interest of existentialist theology was focused on man, and its guiding hermeneutical principle was the individual's question about himself, about the possibility of living authentically. This was a departure from the traditional exposition of the gospel, which was objectified supernaturally and in which faith appeared to degenerate into assent to certain saving facts. In existentialist interpretation, however, the subjectivity of the inquirer was injected into the hermeneutical process, where it brought its preunderstanding of life into play. Only what was appropriated existentially, what was relevant for my life, could pass for understanding. This preunderstanding of what it is that constitutes life was supposed to be criticized and

transformed in the encounter with the subject matter of the
New Testament. The movement in which a new faith and
understanding arises from the preunderstanding by means
of encounter with the text was described as the "hermeneutical circle."

Political theology begins with a modified preunderstanding. Its guiding hermeneutical principle is the question of
authentic life for all men. That does not mean that the question about individual existence must be suppressed or thrust
aside as nonessential. But surely even that question can be
answered only in terms of social conditions and in the context of social hopes. No one can be saved alone. Subjectivity
is injected into even this process of social understanding,
but not for the purpose of seeking understanding and faith
for itself alone; rather it believes in and calls for the indivisible salvation of the whole world. Only what is appropriated and mediated politically, only what is relevant to the
life of everyone in society, can be regarded as understanding. This preunderstanding of a possible life for all men in
society is criticized and transformed by its encounter with
the message of the gospel.

This preunderstanding of political theology includes the
affirmation that the social situation is in principle intelligible and therefore potentially transformable. Changes in
social conditions enable the transformation of men; certain
patterns of behavior—competition, the burden of having to
achieve, the appeal to transitory status symbols—can be
eliminated if the environment no longer reinforces such
behavior. It is certainly incorrect if—in our alienation from
the older, individualistic hopes of men, which were dependent upon "conversion"—we think that institutions "create"

man and that transformation of social structures is all that is necessary to bring forth the new man. From a critical perspective this can be stated only negatively: Under certain social conditions the possibility of liberated and liberating activity is virtually excluded. There are situations that systematically destroy the mother-child relationship; there are ways of organizing labor that define the relation of the strong to the weak on a Darwinian model; and qualities like helpfulness, compassion, or fairness are allowed to waste away because they hinder production. If the conditions are changed, if the situation becomes worthy of being human, if forms of organization encourage cooperation, then the conditions are present for the possibility of a new life; no more, but also no less.

Today this conviction that society can be transformed cannot be abandoned any more than Bultmann could have abandoned the critical, nonmythological understanding of the nexus of natural science. As one who used electric lights and was therefore served by technology, Bultmann was not prepared to accept on faith a three-storied mythological world view. But is it any less mythological to imagine that wars, hunger, and conditions that intensify our world's neuroses are simply determined by fate? Can we ourselves, precisely in line with Bultmann's intention, become involved in pushing birth control, while letting social mythologies such as the necessary suffering of certain classes or the necessary alienation of labor go unchallenged? Because our world no longer shares this preunderstanding of social fate, ideological criticism takes the place of demythologization for us. Hence the conviction that society can be transformed cannot engage in a false statement of the question by asking which conditions are alterable and which are not. This boundary is constantly shifting, and in each case challenges anew the capacities to transcend it.

Today we can no longer consider the conditions that shape our life—as they are exhibited in class, race, heredity, sex, talent, or lifelike happenstance—as a fateful web from which faith redeems us. Such faith necessarily lifts man out of the world, because under these assumptions the only possible sphere of freedom is far removed from the concreteness of everyday life. This understanding of faith as taking man out of the world is tied to the preunderstanding that situations and structures are governed by fate (supra, pp. 33 ff). A theology that understands itself apolitically will attempt to portray the gospel independently of this horizon of social transformations, which for us is indispensable. It makes as a preliminary demand the surrender of social, political reason, which regards the world as transformable. A theology like Bultmann's will view history as having come to an end and will always interpret redemption as escape from the world.

It makes a difference whether Jesus, speaking in John's Gospel about a life full of trials, doubts, and fear, says, "It is finished," or whether this statement is recast in a religious education book as one that may be imitated without cost at any time. This latter interpretation demands the abandonment of our preunderstanding, because it asserts that transformation is no longer necessary.

> If we ask about the future of man, the Bible points to this center. . . . On the cross he said, "It is finished" (John 19:30). Nothing new and exciting can take place in the world any longer. Whatever may come to pass, whatever may happen is not decisive for the world and for men.

> Sickness and war, hunger and need, fortune and profit,
> success and progress can befall us. But they can change
> neither the world nor men.[4]

Even this seemingly purely theological statement contains massive political implications. The offering of verbal solutions hinders genuine transformation. Sensitivity to suffering is stifled; a hidden brutalization is allowed to exist with the tacit support of theology. Consciousness of the possibility that life can break down, the consciousness of tragedy, is destroyed, and the result is a loss in humanity. The pre-understanding that informs all of this is no longer that of our world; the interpretation of faith as escape from the world cannot hold up against ideological criticism.

This does not, however, make ideological criticism the sole valid standard for theology, but only a necessary corrective for theological expressions, which are now to be scrutinized for their social implications, which for the most part are unconscious. If ideological criticism were to become a court before which theology had to justify itself, then society would become the absolute basis and theology would prove unnecessary. But the method followed here attempts to use ideological criticism as a means of freeing the substance of the gospel from its disguises. It becomes an instrument of self-criticism for theology; and with its help the absolute basis that transcends the social order, namely, the gospel (in Bultmann's language, the kerygma), can become free once again from its illusory, destructive, systematic fixations.

---

4. *Die Gottesbotschaft: Ein biblisches Lese- und Arbeitsbuch,* ed. H. D. Bastian and H. Kremers (Düsseldorf: Verlag Bagel, 1965), 2: 194.

THE POLITICAL JESUS

Social awareness of transformation cannot and need not be justified biblically. It is meaningless to ask whether Jesus would directly intervene to transform social conditions. Here we must proceed on the basis of Melanchthon's dictum that the important thing is to know Christ's benefits, not his nature: *Id est Christum cognoscere ejus beneficia cognoscere, non ejus naturas.* Transferred to the present theological discussion, this axiom would have to read as follows: It is not a matter of compiling in a biblicistic sense materials pertaining to the political activity of Jesus and using them to establish whether or not he was a revolutionary. The main thing is not to describe his concrete behavior and imitate it, but rather to discern the intention or tendency of that behavior and to realize anew his goals in our world. Thus it is meaningless to ask: Was Jesus a revolutionary? Where did he stand on violence, on landed property? Instead, we as his friends who affirm the intention of his decision must attempt for our part to declare where we stand today on revolution, property, or violence. This function of his on our behalf (his *beneficia*) is more important than the words and deeds discoverable by the historian, which lead only to imitation, not to discipleship.

Jesus of Nazareth neither analyzed nor criticized the structural conditions under which tax collectors became tax collectors and prostitutes became prostitutes. He received human beings without asking who might have induced them to become tax collectors and prostitutes. He could not ask this question, because—in Marxist terminology—the means of production had not developed to the point where the restructuring of society was technically possible. It is ahistorical and therefore pre-Marxist to ask the New Testament, an antique document, whether it embraces the conviction that social conditions are transformable. It makes no difference whether this question is intended as a criticism of Jesus by Joachim Kahl, or whether, out of an affirmation of existing conditions, it is posed by fundamentalist theologians to discredit political theology. The basis for transformation in the broad sense that we conceive it today was simply not available at that time. But now that it is available, we can no longer retreat behind the questions that thereby emerge. We cannot allow ourselves to neglect the reasons why chemists work in the munitions industry or young men prefer military service to the Peace Corps.

In the hermeneutical process this contemporary pre-understanding that structures can be transformed is confronted by the gospel and thereby is criticized, modified, and liberated, but not by any means simply negated. It is within this hermeneutical process that the question about Jesus' relation to the transformation of this world must be reformulated. Even if we deny that Jesus worked for transformation in the explicit sense of deriving the dialectic of the individual and society from social structures, or beginning the process of transformation with changes in property and social relationships, it cannot be overlooked that, in an indirect sense, the manner in which Jesus thought and acted *de facto* broke open and transformed the social structures of the world in which he lived. Thus, in light of the new brotherhood, familiar associations and limitations lose their traditional status as orders of nature (Mark 3:31–35), and there begins an historicizing of human relationships. "Who are my mother and my brothers?" asks Jesus. The

hypostatizations of orders such as family or modes of behavior such as piety are abolished in Jesus' life. "Leave the
dead to bury their own dead" (Matt. 8:22). Even the most
significant of all social classifications, the division of men
according to their level of culture—those who read and
write and are religiously informed versus those who belong
to classes that are culturally and educationally deprived—
is stripped of its dignity and significance. "You are not to
be called rabbi. . . . Call no man your father on earth. . . .
Neither be called masters." Sovereign authority is abolished,
and in place of a society constructed on a patriarchal model
appears one structured according to the spirit of brotherhood. Matt. 23:8–10 indicates that this practice inaugurated
by Jesus was continued by the community. Above all, however, the abolition of the hitherto valid horizon of a religiously defined society of achievement has had obvious
social ramifications. The blind and the lame had no entrance
to the temple, and for them to be healed also meant to be
reincorporated into the religious community. Jesus associated with women, who were religiously and socially ostra-
cized, and he mingled with outcasts. In Jesus' proclamation
there begins an exodus from familiar and traditional structures of authority based on knowledge and achievement
—a proclamation to which those who throughout the history of Christendom have stood in need of an exodus constantly appealed. "You know that in the world, rulers lord it
over their subjects, and their great men make them feel the
weight of authority; but it shall not be so with you" (Matt.
20:25–26 NEB).

What is here expressed prescientifically as a cipher of
liberation can now be articulated scientifically, at least in

part. Today we are able to formulate more precisely the conditions under which authority can be seen through, controlled, and ultimately destroyed.

THE NEW FUNCTIONS OF POLITICAL THEOLOGY

The gospel has to do with freedom for all, or more precisely—since the reality of oppression remains in the picture—its essence is the *liberation* of all. It is concerned with the oppressed, the poor, those who mourn. This concern, this partisanship, is not to be further deduced, for the Bible admonishes us to share this concern for the freedom of all, indeed to make it our own most distinctive concern. Only the liberation of all can be a valid liberation for the individual; only the happiness of all merits the unconditional affirmation that transcends momentary achievements, which is the meaning of the word "faith." In faith we posit the liberation of all; in the act of faith all of our powers—thinking and feeling, working and waiting—are concentrated on this liberation. We recall the liberation that was experienced earlier and we anticipate that which is yet to come.

Political theology as reflection on faith must give attention to the social situation of those who are brutalized and uncover the social roots of their brutalization. It cannot accomplish this by telling a man out of the blue, "God loves you!" Because all reality is worldly and inherently social, even this statement must be interpreted politically; it has meaning only when it intends the transformation of the status quo. Suppose this is addressed to a man who has lived for fifteen years in the slums of our cities. The contempt that he has suffered makes such a statement incredible to him and leaves him unable to believe in the love of

God. He has learned that he remains unemployed because
he comes from a housing project, or that his children,
though as talented as others, are consigned to inferior
schools. The society that has refused to accept him has,
through the experiences of his life, established itself as such
a monstrous enemy that the situation cannot be glossed
over with a mere word. The capacity to love and to trust
someone is bound to the history and the experiences that
one has undergone. Thus, social conditioning can make it
impossible for the individual to decide whether to trust or
distrust. Social factors have laid hold of him, and he cannot
embrace faith, hope, or love without first being healed.
John's Gospel tells of the pool at Bethesda where invalids
await an angel to stir the water. The first to climb into the
water after it moves is healed. Jesus talks with a sick man
who has been waiting for many years. He is not in a position to enter the water and says to Jesus: "Sir, I have no
man to put me into the pool when the water is troubled"
(John 5:7). As long as he must talk that way he is alone
and therefore helpless and condemned to a life of sickness.
Without other men he has no chance. His illness, whether
it be physical or social—and these are much more closely
related in the New Testament than our modern conceptions
allow for—is not his private affair with which he must deal
alone; it is rather brought into a social context which poses
a question to other men. Jesus puts an end to the situation
in which one must say "I have no man" by putting an end
to the isolation that is both the consequence and the cause
of affliction. In this story healing means: not having to say
any longer "I have no man."

However, if the gospel restores sickness and healing to

their original social context, if it makes the sickness of the sick the sickness of Jesus, from which he finally dies, and if it links the healing of one to that of another, then the language of the gospel as the language of liberation must at the same time have a critical function. The gospel is inconceivable without critical analysis, without "law." The tradition of biblical criticism is to be appropriated and given new life in our social circumstances as a criticism of religion, authority, and society. Association with the prophetic tradition encourages and motivates theology toward a comparable stance. Nevertheless, it would be false to view political theology in its critical function merely as the religious elevation of a scientific-rational criticism. The gospel affords no such elevations, but it surely pushes purely rational or functional projects in a specific direction, toward the liberation of all.

Our problem today is no longer the undisguised but the hidden forms of exploitation, which conceal themselves among apparent freedoms, for example, the freedom to consume whenever, wherever, and in whatever quantity possible. The exploitation concealed there challenges the function of the gospel to unconceal and to accuse (*apocalyptein*). Indeed the gospel heightens consciousness of suffering and dissatisfaction with what has already been achieved. Political theology prods men to combat their own apathy, creating new anguish and inspiring new projects. It entices them to seek transformation. Criticism and enticement, duty and gift, demand and consolation, law and gospel, are directed to the one who is addressed; they accommodate themselves to men, for whom they exist.

6. Truth as Faith's Theory of Praxis

But what is the underlying conception of truth in a political hermeneutic, and how is it related to the understanding of truth in existentialist theology?

The notion of truth that Bultmann develops, primarily in connection with the Gospel of John, bears the stamp of his critique of Greek and idealistic thought. Bultmann divorces himself from a formal understanding of truth such as the disclosure of that-which-is, or the conceptualization of reality (the *adequatio rei et intellectus*), or even the veracity of modern subjectivism.[1] If any of these conceptions of truth were proved correct, then truth would consist of the "teaching about God transmitted by Jesus"—a *theōrein* to which man finds himself related, which he can investigate from a distance, which furnishes him a detached perspective, and which he finally can "know." As Bultmann interprets John, however, the relation to truth cannot be the theoretical relation of the detached observer, because in substance this truth is itself the life that one searches for

1. Cf. Rudolf Bultmann, *Theology of the New Testament,* trans. Kendrick Grobel (New York: Scribner's, 1965), 2: 18–19.

and believes can be the object of contemplation. By accept-
ing truth man surrenders himself in terms of his old projects and opinions. This happens because he "has to take the
way to it for himself." This movement toward truth cannot
be reduced to scientific thought, "for only on the way does
this truth disclose itself."[2] Truth is not taught and then
accepted, but lived and practiced.

The expressions "on the way," "living," and "doing" stand
in critical opposition to the Greek and idealistic traditions
and point to what we today call theory-praxis, even though
Bultmann's ecclesiastical fixation again represses this theoretical-practical tendency. For example, his initial interpretation of the saying of Jesus in Matt. 10:39 ("He who finds
his life will lose it, and he who loses his life for my sake
will find it") is entirely consistent: "The truth of this
statement is not yet realized when it is only comprehended
as general truth."[3] From that it should have been concluded
that this statement becomes true when the meaning of
"life" at any particular time is indicated; in other words, it
becomes true when "life" is lived concretely and situation-
ally, that is, when it is brought into a political context. In
the official ecclesiastical structure of West Germany, for
example, "life" has been interpreted as the church tax collected by the state. Hierarchies and bureaucracies desire to
maintain this life of a bygone era. Another example: Devel-
opmental assistance given to German industry understands
"life" to be big business, whose markets must be preserved.

2. Rudolf Bultmann, *The Gospel of John*, trans. G. R. Beasley-Murray,
et al. (Philadelphia: Westminster, 1971), p. 606.
3. Rudolf Bultmann, *History and Eschatology: The Presence of Eternity* (New York: Harper Torchbook, 1962), p. 151.

Or in the private sphere: A mother clings tenaciously to her children in whom she has her "life." She refuses to let them grow up. But if the political horizon is essential, then we must go beyond individual fate and ask who might have given the mother the idea that her life exists in her children. Who taught her that, who manipulated her with such propaganda and made her so dependent on the clichés of society? The political context is thus necessary for the truth to become concrete. Bultmann, to be sure, solves the problem of how a general truth is realized, not by its becoming concrete but in a purely formal sense, because he alters the form in which truth is communicated. "For man cannot say this word to himself [why not?—he can surely read it!], it must be said to him—always individually to you and to me. Just this is the meaning of the Christian message."[4] But it makes no sense to free general truths from their petrification if we merely change the speaker, the location, and the volume; truth can be realized not simply by being spoken, but only by becoming a concrete reality in society.

Nevertheless, Bultmann's critical stance opposing the merely theoretical relation to truth is indeed interesting because he exhibits a strange kinship to Karl Marx, who in his "Theses on Feuerbach" also established the relation of man to truth on a new, non-idealistic base, namely, that of theory and praxis. For him there is no such thing as a truth that can be acquired in detached, contemplative observation; the relation to truth—as in the case of Bultmann—is determined by its interest in life. Marx says in the second thesis: "In praxis man must prove the truth, that is, the

4. Ibid.

actuality and power and this-sidedness, of his thinking."[5]
Political theology enters precisely here, because it grasps
the relation to truth no longer as one of contemplation and
theory only, as accords with the Greek mind, but as an
operative and practical relation found not only in John but
even more in the proclamation of Jesus.

THE OPERATIVE-PRACTICAL RELATION TO TRUTH

For the sake of the question of truth, therefore, we must
agree with Metz's contention that the fundamental hermeneutical problem of theology is "not, properly speaking, the
problem of how systematic theology stands in relation to
historical theology, how dogma stands in relation to history,
but what the relation is between theory and praxis, between
understanding the faith and social praxis."[6] This new relation of theory and praxis does not mean that word disinte-
grates into sheer activism. But there can be no doubt that
word and situation are bound together more securely than
in a nonpolitical theology. The "purely" kerygmatic word
that is totally independent of the situation has no relation
to praxis; to the contrary, even the public, spoken word of
the sermon can embody a possible fragment of social praxis,
which can be tested by the conflicts that it provokes.

When Grässer argues in this context that the theological
left appropriates uncritically as a science of action the
Marxist conception of theory and praxis,[7] we must ask him

5. Karl Marx, *Writings of the Young Marx on Philosophy and Society,*
trans. L. D. Easton and K. H. Guddat (New York: Doubleday, 1967),
p. 401. (Translation altered.)
6. J. B. Metz, *Theology of the World,* trans. William Glen-Doepel
(New York: Herder & Herder, 1969), p. 112. (Translation altered.)
7. Erich Grässer, "Die politische Herausforderung an die biblische
Theologie," *Evangelische Theologie,* 30 (1970): 235.

to clarify the understanding of truth with which he proceeds and to justify an understanding of truth totally void of praxis. Furthermore, contrary to Grässer's uncritical assumption, the Marxist understanding of truth does not by any means lead to blind activism.[8] Habermas interprets the Marxian understanding of truth as follows:

> The unity of theory and praxis signifies the truth that is to be established and, conjointly, the supreme standard of reason, since within the situation of alienation all efforts that move toward the establishment of truth are already seen as rational. Reason is the entry into future truth.[9]

From a theological point of view, it is indeed problematic whether the conception of reason presented here, if it has been freed from its theological roots and implications, is possible and whether it would not be more appropriate to say: "Faith is the entry into future truth." But that adds nothing to the understanding of theory and praxis; what really matters is the "entry into future truth,"[10] in which, theoretically at least, theology cooperates with other disci-

8. How, generally speaking, the Protestant discussion of the substance of political theology descends to a disgraceful level is best characterized by Helmut Thielicke's moving question, "Can structures be converted?" ("Können sich Strukturen bekehren?" *Zeitschrift für Theologie und Kirche,* 66 [1969]: 98–114.) In essence, only the Catholic discussion wrestles seriously with the problem, and this is true not only of the critics of political theology (Hans Maier, Karl Lehmann) but also of its proponents (J. B. Metz, Frank Böckle, W. Oelmüller, K. Rahner), all of whom have published essays in the volume edited by H. Peukert, *Diskussion zur "politischen Theologie"* (Mainz/Munich: Chr. Kaiser/Grünewald, 1969).

9. J. Habermas, *Theorie und Praxis,* vol. 2 of *Politica* (Berlin: Luchterhand, 1963), p. 316.

10. Cf. also Jürgen Moltmann, "Toward a Political Hermeneutic of the Gospel," *Religion, Revolution, and the Future,* trans. M. Douglas Meeks (New York: Scribner's, 1969), pp. 83–107.

plines. That presupposes a non-perfectionistic understanding of faith (or as the opponents of political theology would
say, a certain "re-Judaizing" of faith).

Obviously the concept of "entry into future truth" formulated by Habermas contains more of eschatology than it
does of existentialist interpretation, which seeks to attain its
concretion not through social mediation but only through
"proclamation." Political theology, however, grounds its
understanding of truth in the still undisclosed unity of
theory and praxis. From the gospel it obtains the nonderivable promise and the demand for peace, freedom, and
justice for all people. It functions, therefore, both critically
and constructively, engaging in ideological criticism and
projecting innovative models, and both tasks are grounded
in the theory-praxis model that is evident in Jesus' message
and in his life and death. Truth as it is meant here cannot
tolerate abstraction, naked theory, pure doctrine, or the
abrupt, unexpected, and therefore dogmatic kerygma. The
truth of Christ exists only as concrete realization, which
means: the verification principle of every theological statement is the praxis that it enables for the future. Theological
statements contain as much truth as they deliver practically
in transforming reality. "Reality" is not understood in this
context simply as a given balance of power, and "transform" is not to be taken exclusively in the activistic sense.
The statement "your sins are forgiven," for example, can
void the reality of the individual, the reality determined
by his past, but it can possess this transforming power only
if he who utters it has shared in the transformation, only if
he makes restitution for the past with its accumulation of
guilt and has divested himself of all magical expectations of

words. The statement "you are called to freedom" becomes true for wage earners not when they hear it proclaimed, but when it becomes a concrete social actuality: you are called to be self-determining, to cooperate, to organize your own work. Their reality is transformed because they acquire a new understanding of who they are. The statement "you shall be my people" becomes true if it affects the consumers, manufacturers, and salesmen of napalm; if, therefore, it opens men's eyes to their role in destroying the very life that was promised to all men together.

From a Christian point of view, theory and praxis can be understood today only in their unity, which means truth is not something that we find or by which we are found, but something that we make true. Only such a creative understanding of truth is suitable for faith; the quest for the verification principle for theological statements is the scientific and theoretical consequence of this way of thinking.

THE ABANDONMENT OF PRAXIS TO INSTRUMENTAL REASON

This operative-practical understanding of truth, however, has been obliterated in the retrogression from Bultmann's own position, and even the "future unity" of theory and praxis has been shattered in kerygmatic neoorthodoxy. This theology has its theory in the doctrine of justification, while its praxis is usually described with devotional fervor as "certainly a fruit and outgrowth of right Christian belief, but not its sole essence or act."[11] At the same time, however, its praxis is anxiously limited by a faith which "neither arises from, nor consists in" the transformation of situations.

11. G. Harbsmeier, "Das Experiment als Gottesdienst—Liturgie der Revolution?" *Verkündigung und Forschung*, 15 (1970): 14.

Here faith is purely theoretical, the acceptance of doctrine. What remains is *caritas* or, more precisely stated, the abandonment of praxis to a reason that is glorified idealistically as "perceptive," or technocratically as "unbiased," but still a reason that never questions its goals. This kind of reason Horkheimer and Habermas have appropriately classified as "instrumental reason."[12]

What instrumental reason is—namely, reason that is no longer concerned with goals and final objectives, but only with the best rational methods—is illustrated very clearly by the behavior of U.S. troops in Vietnam. In guerrilla warfare the conventional army needs information about the place, number, and plans of its intangible foe, and it is necessary for the survival of its own soldiers to acquire this information. It can be obtained only from Vietcong prisoners, who surrender it only under torture. Instrumental reason compels the Americans to refrain from inflicting the torture themselves (which happens only in special units), but they stand by with tape recorders in hand while the South Vietnamese supervise the torment. In view of this inevitable practice of instrumental reason, there is a certain naïveté in abandoning the praxis of faith to such a loosely defined reason, which perhaps no longer glorifies rulers as "authorities" but still honors the irrational economic system as the most effective instrument of force. Above all, however, the fulfillment of life in faith is destroyed by this abandonment because men are no longer given the freedom and the courage to risk their lives for

12. Cf. M. Horkheimer, *Vernunft und Selbsterhaltung*, vol. 7 of *Aus der Reihe* (Frankfurt: S. Fischer Verlag, 1970), and M. Horkheimer, *Eclipse of Reason* (New York: Oxford University Press, 1947).

future truth. The biblical message in which theory and praxis were related to each other like faith, hope, and love has been supplanted in ecclesiastical neoorthodoxy by pure doctrine devoid of praxis, by doctrine that abandons praxis to instrumental reason, which even Luther knew was a whore. Instrumental reason, which functions perfectly according to its technical laws, "can certainly rationalize social and political praxis *within* a particular nexus of ends and means,"[13] but it cannot consider adequately its so-called preferences for the objectives it pursues; rather, like a whore, it will make these decisions according to the price.

Even when the concept of truth is no longer grounded in the unity of theory and praxis, it is still possible to make a case for the Christian's responsibility toward the world; but this is not viewed as political theology but at most as a "consequence" of faith.[14] Thus we must criticize this concept of responsibility as inadequate, for it is based upon existing structures that at best are only partially distorted —for example, by egotistic individuals—but it never affects the structures themselves. It seems to me that serious theological questions arise when love is stripped of its power by viewing it as a "consequence" of faith, by reducing it to a secondary effect. Such a reduction betrays the unity of theory and praxis not only for the future, but shatters it even for the present. This "consequence" has nothing to do with that political and theological reflection for which practical reason surrenders itself in obedience to Christ (2 Cor. 10:5).

13. J. B. Metz, *Theology of the World*, p. 152.
14. Cf. Erich Grässer, "Die politische Herausforderung," p. 238. See also p. 247 where, betraying a naïve trust in instrumental reason, he speaks of the "impartiality of the relation to the world."

A statement by Schmithals seems to be a case in point: "The civil war in Biafra cannot be ended by 'the church,' whereas it would have ended long ago if the Christian leaders on both sides had taken their faith more seriously."[15] This kind of churchly responsibility for the world can be characterized as a totally unsuspecting, apolitically conceived moralism. The war broke out when the oil companies, which had prospected in the Nigerian delta, switched their payment of royalties from Gowon to Ojukwu. They hastened the secession, because it was easier to gain access to the incredibly cheap oil (cheap because it could easily be refined and transported) in tiny Biafra than in huge Nigeria. Half a nation starved for the sake of their business interests—and this is political information that must be taken into account. It seems to be the case that an economic system based on competition between private firms has a definite proclivity toward war. We can hardly reproach the oil companies, or even the expendable generals for looking after their own interests, because it is contradictory to the spirit of instrumental reason simply to abandon the cheapest oil to the competition. Political theology takes this network of information into consideration; it is not the naïve moralism of a country preacher berating the evil world, which in other respects is left in the care of instrumental reason. The understanding of truth in political theology, which is based on the future or eschatological unity of theory and praxis, must resist this abandonment of praxis to instrumental reason; otherwise, the feeling of having been abandoned, of being powerless, will be suggested to men.

15. W. Schmithals, *Das Christuszeugnis in der heutigen Gesellschaft* (Hamburg: Herbert Reich Verlag, 1970), p. 32.

Sometimes this happens in a consciously ideological fashion because man's sense of being dependent on grace is used as a form of legalism to discredit his own initiative. But it also occurs psychologically because the isolation of man conditioned by the structures of modern capitalism is transfigured theologically: the oft-repeated statement that by our power surely nothing will be accomplished conforms ultimately to that situation. The political consequences of such feelings of powerlessness are well known from the history of national socialism, namely, a sudden intoxication with omnipotence and the creation of irrational political structures. Is it an untheological accident that the electoral potential of the neo-Nazi National German Party lies in the isolated, rural Protestant areas of Franconia and Hesse?

7. Sin, Politically Interpreted

Political theology arises from an understanding of truth that stresses the inseparable unity of the theory and praxis of faith; accordingly, the task of theology is to bear upon the structures of the present-day world and to examine its assertions in light of their social relevance. Political theology cannot engage in severing a theory of faith, as the superior component, from a praxis of love that has value only as an apparent consequence of faith, because it conceives truth not as knowledge, but as fulfillment of life.

Thus the antithesis to the truth lived in Christ—unbelief or sin—must also be reflected in its theoretical-practical understanding, which means that it must be politicized. It seems to me that the most fundamental *dissensus* dividing theological generations and camps, though still scarcely thematized, lies in a new, essentially political interpretation of sin. Nowhere is a Word-of-God theology distinguished more clearly from a political interpretation of the gospel than in its underlying conception of sin. To be sure, the theological right imputes to political theology the unrestrained arrogance of an "abolition of sin through the transformation of conditions."[1] In reality, it appears to me that

1. G. Harbsmeier, "Das Experiment als Gottesdienst—Liturgie der Revolution?" *Verkündigung und Forschung*, 15 (1970): 15.

a different quality of seriousness and a profound understanding of sin is present wherever the hope exists that by
specific changes in social structures the number of forces
compelling us to sin today can be decreased.

"NATURAL MAN" IN MODERN CAPITALISM

What kinds of forces are these and what have they to do
with the individual? I shall mention some examples: With
every banana I eat, I am defrauding those who grow them
of the greater part of their wages and abetting the United
Fruit Company in its plunder of Latin America. The tenant
who grits his teeth and pays the mandatory rent increase is
helping objectively to swell the ranks of those banished to
a homeless existence in the slums; they are sacrificed for the
sake of our rights to property and land. The German pastor
lets his salary be paid by people who have never been
asked whether they need or want a pastor. The manufac-
turer keeps extravagant machinery in operation by turning
out products that last only a short time. The physician pre-
scribes cheaper medicine for welfare patients. Such matters
of fact are commonly regarded as stimuli of the industrial-
ized world. We cannot act in ways other than those prescribed for us; we must adapt to them objectively. Our
behavior is then frequently promoted to the most important
virtue; we are forced to cooperate with the system that
presupposes and reproduces such matters of fact. In developed societies there are no "great" refusals—contra Herbert
Marcuse—but at most individual refusals with specific
goals. These do not essentially involve the economic entanglement of our profits with the misery of others, because
even in the best of cases they are only indirectly politically

effective. Even the American draft resister who burned his draft card remained entangled in the economic structures of the system. We cannot escape our world.

What does that mean theologically? Do such facts lend themselves to theological interpretation? Do their social origins and their consequences for the individual who is exposed to them have anything to do with what the Bible calls sin? The consciousness thus confronted resists this interpretation by referring precisely to unalterable necessity. It is not ready to admit to such a biblical interpretation of our life or else wants to limit it to private existence. Theology is dominated by a depoliticized understanding of sin, and the collectives in which we live—nations, races, classes, communities, groups—do not enter the picture. To be sure it does concede a theological interpretation of our world's fallen state insofar as that interpretation remains metaphysical and ahistorical and is emptied of all concrete reality. This theological interpretation is repudiated to the extent that it attaches itself as criticism to the real contradictions of society. Therefore this consciousness finds it easy to develop defense mechanisms against such a theological-political interpretation, by means of which sin is defined as what has "always been the case."

But which consciousness is it that talks this way and sets up defense mechanisms? Is it not the "natural man"—the man who is unaware of his own misery, who understands himself as guiltless, who is incapable of noticing the suffering of others? This theological term does not refer to an unchangeable essence of man, but to his inimical position that remains unchanged outside of grace, as opposed to that which reveals man to be responsible, free, and capable of guilt. Natural man is dependent on stimuli; indeed, he understands himself as a function of existing forces. He is—here and now—the man shaped by modern capitalism: he hates God, as the tradition expresses it, because he regards interest in profits and preparedness for aggression as unalterable characteristics of man. The basic values of our society (e.g., whoever produces and whoever consumes are good) are taken over as self-evident norms. Even when he suffers under these norms and sees what they do to the defenseless members of society who produce nothing, he remains natural man in the theological sense of the word. He is the man who wants to know nothing of sin, since for him the world has been forgiven and is, therefore, to be accepted as is. He cannot understand it as a *laboratorium possibilitis salutis* (Ernst Bloch). His world, from which he has no distance, defines him only in terms of his capacities to produce and to consume. Everything that lies beyond this reality is left in an intangible, fateful darkness, while perceivable reality has already been privately interpreted. The privatization of consciousness and the experience of powerlessness play into each other's hands.

ON THE CONCEPT OF ORIGINAL SIN

Is this natural self-understanding to be designated as sin? Rudolf Bultmann says the Christian understanding of original sin means "that we always enter our present as those attempting to succeed on our own, that we come from a history and stand in a world that has been all along and still is governed by a particular understanding of human relations, and that this understanding governs us from the start: everyone should seek what is his; no one should pay

serious attention to the others."[2] The terms that Bultmann
uses to designate sin (wanting to hold one's own, succeed-
ing on one's own, securing one's own life, clinging to that
which is at one's disposal, securing a claim by achievement,
clinging to oneself)[3] are rooted in the bourgeois-capitalist
world and its criteria of achievement; they can hardly apply
to existentialist-ontological structures, but must instead be
verified in their historical context. We know, for example,
from the works of Margaret Mead that societies have ex-
isted which had no civilization in our sense and were not
even aware of sociopsychological pressures "to succeed on
one's own" as described by Bultmann. Such knowledge does
not temper the biblical concept of sin, but only renders it
historically more intelligible. It is possible to conceive of
societies in which the pressures to "succeed on one's own"
are reduced. This fact does not eliminate our feeling of
guilt but rather intensifies it, because we no longer understand merely our individual role in the matter—i.e., in
making profits based on the exploitation of the weak—and
because we no longer view the collective inability to change
this situation as an unavoidable fate, but must see the social
order as one chosen by us in the social world that we have
established. Comparative ethnology and sociology extend
theoretically the sphere of perceptible freedom, which
means in practice for Christian consciousness that they
teach us to recognize more precisely the extent to which
we are sinners. The presupposition of this knowledge is

2. Rudolf Bultmann, *Glauben und Verstehen*, 4 vols. (Tübingen,
J. C. M. Mohr [Paul Siebeck], 1933–65), 2:14.
3. Ibid.; *History and Eschatology* (New York, 1957), pp. 99, 150;
Ibid.; *Glauben und Verstehen*, 3:210.

that the collective past becomes answerable and that this inheritance is taken over as one's own history through identification with the world in which we live. Only on the basis of
this identification, which means the assumption of guilt,
can distance and criticism arise; criticism of the existing
world without identifying with it leads to apolitical escapism, such as that found in the hippy communes of California. Those who flee civilization believe they are innocent
and nonparticipating; they would save their own souls from
corruption. Only when the individual's existence is portrayed no longer as "squatting abstractly outside the world"
(Marx) but as grounded in social relationships—only then
will it be possible to appropriate our own world in the consciousness of freedom.

The theological understanding of sin underlying all this
embraces compulsion and freedom at the same time. I have
not selected this world for myself, I have been born into it.
Every historical understanding of man is constituted by his
bondage to the past; there is no zero point at which he
could begin, for at every point he is already stamped by
and grounded in the world from which he comes. At the
same time, however, freedom is presupposed in the concept
of original sin, which means that man has the capacity for
guilt. I collaborate with what has already been placed at
my disposal; there is an "I" which acts, regardless of
whether the action is aggressive or passive, and which has
intentionally conceived diverse possibilities of behavior. We
must think of compulsion and freedom, "inheritance" and
sin, as standing in a dialectical relation to each other—not
as rigid, contradictory antitheses excluding one another,
but as a contradiction present in reality itself. This con-

tradiction causes suffering for men who become aware of
it, and it drives them to discover new forms that resolve
the contradiction. From a theological point of view, the
contradiction between the inheritance from a world already there and the sin of accommodation to it arouses a
desire that is no longer content with the forgiveness of individual sins. The contradiction can be resolved only by a
renewal of the whole man in a new world.

SIN AS COLLABORATION

In this understanding the sinner is the collaborator
(seemingly harmless from the point of view of the natural
consciousness) of a structurally founded, usually anony-
mous injustice. Accordingly, for political theology sin would
be collaboration and apathy. If these are to be recognized,
theology must have the help of the human sciences, insofar
as they provide information about the possibilities of alternative behavior.

Conservative theology's fear of sociology is therefore a
defense mechanism that is used to preserve an innocuous
consciousness of sin. The Protestant consciousness of sin is
innocuous and distresses no one in its indiscriminate univer-
ality, for it identifies sin, not theoretically but *de facto*, with
a universal human fate comparable perhaps to smallpox,
against which we are protected by vaccination. The experiences of Luther become a welcomed alibi. Severed from
a psychosocial background, freed from the compulsion to
make confession, purged of suicidal fantasies, man experiences a global but diffuse feeling which religiously and
politically is more like powerlessness than sin in the strict
sense of the word, meaning something inseparable from

freedom. Neither social criticism nor self-criticism, not to mention criticism of the church, can be developed out of this unworldly concept of sin that concerns only God and the individual soul. On this basis Ernst Bloch's criticism of a "particularly tall" myth is to be understood as applying to Bultmann, namely, "the heteronomous arch-myth of the Fall, according to which man must first be delivered from himself, even now, when *Deus pro nobis* has appeared."[4] That is certainly a misunderstanding of Bultmann, who has reflected on the dialectic of other-determination and self-determination, but it does illuminate Bultmann's apparent understanding of sin, which has not been elucidated from a social perspective and has therefore been decreed heteronomous. Bultmann has hardly freed himself from the non-discriminating Protestant tradition of powerlessness and, accordingly, of the devaluation of all man's activity and creativity. He has even reinforced it by appropriating a pair of Heideggerian concepts, "disposable" and "not disposable," because it turns out that these concepts are so similar to the Pauline *sarx* and *pneuma*. If the latter expressed primarily a direction of the will, the vital intention of self-certainty and self-surrender, they nevertheless become—especially in Bultmann's anti-institutional polemic—more and more substantial, such that spontaneity is always spiritually effective and not at our disposal, whereas organization and plan are always fleshly and sinful. Granted that it is correct for individuality to be conceived essentially in the I-Thou relation, nevertheless, for concrete individuality, which lives in the fullness of social

4. Ernst Bloch, *Atheism in Christianity*, trans. J. T. Swann (New York: Herder and Herder, 1972), p. 41.

relationships, that which is apparently undisposed has by no means been disposed by God, but long ago by others. Christian openness to the future is not demonstrated by our not disposing (the French say it better, *laissez faire*), but by establishing within society a certain latitude whereby the future can become manifest as something not purchased by propaganda, production, and achievement.

The political interpretation of the Bible has an interest in making sure that a sense of sin is not supplanted by a feeling of powerlessness. The powerlessness forced upon us religiously only conceals our sins, our profit, and our apathy. Here we shall adhere to the Old Testament content of the word *sin*, which in all of its diverse meanings refers "primarily . . . not to individual, private sentiments, but to the connection between the deed that disturbs the divinely willed union of brotherhood, and the resulting punishment."[5] Protest against God and against a sociopolitical failure are not dissociated any more than man's action is dissociated from his state of being in the understanding of ancient Israel. For us today—after the demise of the immediate, religious relationship to God—this means: God can be hated and given offense only in man. Sin is not to be understood in a special religious sense as the lack of love for God or as rebellion against a master, but it must be thought of in worldly and political categories. Neither the desecrated temple nor the declining churches are our accusers, but the situation of our world.

Having begun today with the political-theological point

5. W. D. Marsch, "Is Consciousness of Sin False Consciousness?" in *Moral Evil under Challenge*, ed. J. B. Metz, *Concilium* (New York: Herder & Herder, 1970), p. 30.

of view of the Old Testament, we ought not to consider the history of individuation carried further in the New Testament as retrogressive, but the depoliticizing of the Pauline understanding of sin, which relates sin to God so much in terms of self-certainty, achievement, and pride that the earthly concretions are easily obscured. The individual responsibility of man will not decrease where a political *coram Christo* is discussed. Political theology reveals for the first time the truth of existentialist theology, because it enables and does not merely postulate an existential way of speaking, which also concerns the individual.

If someone asks what a Christian political theology adds to the general movement called the New Left, I would put it this way: It is not enough to criticize property rights and the import duty imposed on manufactured goods from developed countries, so long as we, as "powerless" individuals, are not able to clarify how we are entangled in the general structures, that is, how we profit from the structures and how we conform to the introverted norms that we regard as self-evident—for example, the norms of achievement, consumerism, reasons of state—and pass them on to others, even when we reject them privately and verbally. A criticism of society which does not take account of this introversive mechanism, and which therefore does not detect and give expression to the capitalist or to the concentration camp guard that is in each one of us, but instead creates enemies in hostile projections, I consider political propaganda, plain and simple, and not a political interpretation of the gospel.

8. Forgiveness, Politically Interpreted

"DESPAIR AT NOT WILLING TO BE ONESELF"*

It is always the sins of my nation, my race, and my class (the bourgeois property holders) that Jesus Christ exposes and on account of which he accuses us. He asks what we have done or failed to do for the least of his brothers, and in the face of this question we discover the connection between incapacity and weakness, between hopelessness and blindness. But how can this connection be broken? How can powerlessness be overcome?

As soon as we stop viewing sin simply as a private matter that happens primarily between individuals, within a family, or even among the personal relations at one's place of work, and begin to understand it as an essentially political and social concept, then the question of the forgiveness of sins is also extended into another dimension and is beset with difficulties that cannot be resolved in traditional theological language. A lucid awareness of the social situation is at the same time knowledge that cripples man, who is not born in isolation and who feels as though he has been auctioned off to the situation. His sensitivity for the suffer-

---

*The translation of this heading incorporates a correction based on correspondence with the author.

ing of another has been sharpened, but so has the feeling of having no way out and of inescapable entanglement and collaboration. Therefore it is preferable to deny the possibility of transformation, and a kind of reverse asceticism, which purges itself of work, achievement, consumption, and success, takes the place of an active repentance that could tackle the compromising conditions themselves. Surely in the private sector, the sphere of apparent freedom, we find sympathetic friends who suffer from similar social causes, but in the world of work the total isolation that is built into the system and destroys every attempt at a new beginning is far more prevalent.

Modern capitalism offers the sensitized man a profusion of possibilities for escaping the consequences of his awareness and settling down—though crippled and sold out—in the more comfortable world. Mere knowledge of causes and of their theoretical potential for transformation by no means provides an escape from powerlessness. Even that which becomes intellectually transparent releases no power for real change. What is missing is faith in the possibility of a new beginning, and many find themselves in the position of Nicodemus, who thought it impossible for a man "to be born anew" (John 3), although he had already discovered the necessity of a new birth.

The consciousness of sin in which sin is understood politically drives man to the experience of having no way out, an experience that the churchly, privatistic, innocuous consciousness of sin knows nothing about. This situation, which we experience as politically mediated—namely, the undertow of sin—is precisely formulated by Luther's words: "I fell ever deeper into the mire, and my life was no longer worth anything." Since we continue to collaborate while hopes of transforming petrified relationships run aground and are smashed to bits, we contract a sickness that Kierkegaard has called "despair at not willing to be oneself." This "despair of weakness," which is widely dispersed among diverse classes, is described in the portrait of a man whose residence has become intolerable for some reason or other: "So he leaves it, but he does not move out, he does not engage a new dwelling, he continues to regard the old one as his habitation; he reckons that the offense will pass away. So it is with the despairer."[1]

Kierkegaard analyzes the existential decision that underlies this despair but without examining its social and political origins. In a direct sense, therefore, his category applies to men of another era. In fact, we do not seek "a new dwelling" in which to live, but rather push the despair along before us. "Not willing to be oneself" is the desire of weakness, which must capitulate before the superior power of the structures without admitting it. Kierkegaard renders a theological judgment on this man who experiences himself as powerless and entangled—namely, that it is "despair," therefore the antithesis of faith, which determines him. He does not presume to believe in forgiveness or new life, and the private solution to this universally recognized problem still appears to such despair as the most viable. The step from this despair of weakness to that of revolutionary defiance, in which one "despairs at willing to be oneself," is not taken here.

1. Søren Kierkegaard, *Fear and Trembling and the Sickness unto Death*, trans. Walter Lowrie, (Princeton: Princeton University Press, 1954), pp. 182–194; quotation from p. 189.

THE DIFFICULTY OF BELIEVING IN FORGIVENESS

Is there a way out of this situation of powerlessness? Can even the sins of collaboration and apathy be forgiven? and if so, how, in view of the fact that we continue to collaborate and still regard the old residence as our own? Forgiveness of sins could be a reality only where men break the enslavement to their powerlessness and then are liberated—not as promised by some magical expectation, because that merely replaces one form of bondage with another, but in such a way that we are able to believe in liberation and begin to realize it with one another. But where should this forgiveness, this new beginning, come from if society isolates the individual in all essential problems and in fact knows no forgiveness?

The difficulty of believing in forgiveness in the sense of a new beginning has a parallel in our method of production: increasingly, all products are intentionally designed and manufactured to wear out and be thrown away. Defective products are not repaired, but are consigned to the junk heap. In this industrial situation the acceptance of imperfection, the endeavor to rebuild the damaged article and to give it another chance, is technologically obsolete.[2] The "bruised reed" that is not broken and the dimly burning wick that is not extinguished (Isa. 42:3) become meaningless images under modern conditions of production: the bruised reed is useless junk and the dimly burning wick is replaced. To restore it would be an error and a stupid blunder.

2. Cf. Dorothee Soelle, *Christ the Representative*, trans. David Lewis (Philadelphia: Fortress, 1967), pp. 39–42.

If in 1950 it is considered socially out of the question to own a car, refrigerator, or television set produced in 1947, then fidelity has already been transvalued, having become a vice, the sabotage of production. May we expect John Doe, who is pressured every three years to trade his automobile for a new one, to rest content with the wife he acquired ten or twenty years ago, who was brand new in 1935 but now is totally worn out?[3]

The difficulty of believing in forgiveness today is heightened by the organization of common life in our society. The act of forgiveness is conceivable only as a personal act encompassing everything. God does not forgive some sins while letting others go unforgiven; he forgives the sin of men. In a society constituted by a pluralism of roles, where we act at times only in terms of prescribed conduct, such behavior concerning the whole man has no place and no meaning. Forgiveness can never be realized in terms of conduct prescribed by one's role; it destroys itself whereever it is partially fulfilled. Whoever forgives some things and not others does not truly forgive and denies the new beginning. The impossibility of all partial forgiveness is precisely illustrated by statements like the following: "I would have forgiven him for adultery except that he lied to me—it is all over as far as I am concerned!" Partial forgiveness holds open further humiliation of the guilty party, and maintains its reservations only in order to bring them up again at the appropriate opportunity; it cannot mean a new beginning. In fact, one does not forgive this or that wrong behavior, one forgives a man—without qualification and without reservation. If, however, personal and there-

3. G. Anders, *Philosophische Stenogramme* (Munich: C. H. Beck, 1965), pp. 68–69.

fore total fulfillment are possible only in the most intimate
surroundings of familiar and cordial relationships, outside
of which forgiveness is inconceivable, why should human
beings be able to believe in forgiveness at all, and what is
the source of the inspiration to begin anew?

FORGIVENESS "FROM ABOVE"

The traditional Christian answer to this question is that
God forgives men. Whatever we do to others or fail to do
should be forgiven by God. It is precisely where those
whom we have offended are no longer able to speak that
God should step in and forgive in their place. But this traditional view becomes a real problem as soon as we draw
forgiveness and sin out of their privatistic reduction and
return them once more to concrete social questions.

The fate of ex-Nazis in Germany illustrates how impossible it is to get rid of one's own acknowledged past. Error
and guilt cannot be atoned publicly since there are no
courts and reference groups for that purpose. The public in
a democracy is founded on discussion, argument, and control. In the strict sense of the word, however, there is no
argument for the forgiveness of sin any more than, for example, the repentance felt by a man like Albert Speer,
Hitler's armaments minister, is controllable and can be
subject to objective criteria of examination.[4] His associates
must believe his repentance. What is required is a judgment in favor of the guilty, an advance of trust in him that

4. Cf. E. C. Hirsch, "Gott vergibt—die Öffentlichkeit nicht. Haben
Nazis lebenslänglich?" National German Radio Broadcast, Hannover,
December 13, 1970.

establishes the possibility of a new beginning. But even this judgment can be made only by individuals in our society. Family and perhaps friends can accept the one who has become guilty, but surely it is demanding too much of one's fellow laborers that they should receive the ex-convict. Usually the facts of the case are kept secret from them. There are in our society no courts that review life sentences and make it possible for men to begin anew as was the case earlier in Christian culture. Former Nazis, even those who were less prominent, rarely have any possibilities left, other than private acceptance, especially when they develop a sense of guilt and believe they have gambled away the right to rehabilitation or a career. Society takes revenge on those who do not belittle their role and gloss over their conduct; it hardly knows rehabilitation and certainly not the forgiveness of sin.

In socialist countries accusation and defense, self-criticism and expulsion from the party, expiation, punishment, and reincorporation into the group take place in the collectives and therefore among men who work with each other. Instruments have been created in those societies similar to those of ancient cloisters, which make possible a new beginning for the wayward and the guilty. It is widely known that these instruments are used almost exclusively for brainwashing, so that it is difficult for us to recognize in them the old structures of sin, repentance, absolution, and penance. Conversion that is dependent upon a specific human group can be agonizing and quite legalistic. But in a society that knows only stifling silence for the guilty outside of the legal process, these tendencies of the socialists

appear to me worthy of consideration. In our society
guilt remains unatoned, which means that forgiveness is
impossible.

What does the appeal to God accomplish here? In other
words, can God—independently of whatever "the world,"
and therefore society, does or fails to do—bestow forgiveness directly on a penitent man and make possible a new
beginning for him? What does the word *God* mean in the
above mentioned radio broadcast, "God Forgives, Not the
Public"? Is forgiveness possible apart from the one who has
been offended? Is it conceivable that God forgives behind
the back of those whom it properly concerns? In the Sermon
on the Mount the man who wanted to swindle forgiveness
by entering the temple and bringing his offering to the
altar, thus turning directly to God, is admonished: "Leave
your gift there before the altar and go; first be reconciled
to your brother and then come and offer your gift" (Matt.
5:24). What kind of role could conceivably be played by a
God who acts without mediation? Can he intervene "from
above" and establish peace where none can exist, because
blood and tears and blighted life stand in the way of it?

The difficulty that arises with forgiveness "from above"
is not so much metaphysical—the fact that we refer to a
source of deliverance grounded outside of the one reality
in which we live—as it is historical. When we appeal to
forgiveness "from above," we show sublime contempt for
men who have been stripped of even the minimal right to
offer forgiveness themselves for what may have been done
to them. Those who have died in the gas chambers or from
starvation cannot forgive. Men who with our help have
been cheated of their life, those who have become bitter,

the neurotics, the shattered—none of them can forgive. And a God who settles that debt in their stead, who makes arrangements with us at their expense, is not the God of Jesus who signifies the indivisible salvation of all. Salvation always remains privatistic where it appears as forgiveness "from above."

The traditional Christian schema distinguishes the forgiveness given by God from the conversion that we accomplish in the world. When the second part of the schema is excluded, perhaps because the guilty one is too old or too ill, we become dependent on the first and comfort ourselves with the forgiveness of God. But is it actually bestowed directly, without the mediation of other men? Does this notion of forgiveness, which acknowledges an otherworldly power, not throw men even deeper into doubt and fear, and is the process that never comes to completion not fertile ground for neurosis? The isolation of the individual and his attachment to the supernatural God belong together. Perhaps precisely in the Protestant tradition, which has renounced the old instruments and institutionalizations of forgiveness, we have considered the problem too much in terms of extremes—from the point of view of the dying, of guilt for the dead. All too often forgiveness was limited to the moment in which man is assured of the grace of God; and the continuity with the broader dimensions of life, the real social possibilities of liberated man, were unimportant by comparison. The reduction of the individual to subjectivity and of salvation to the private sphere signify a God who is related only to individuals and then only inwardly and secretly. Forgiveness was not so much liberation for new life as deliverance from old guilt, and thus the moment of forgiveness, isolated as it is from the history of men and from their possible future, is necessarily false and destructive.

"THE ONION"

Conversion or turning about (*Umkehr*) is therefore a clearer word for what is meant by forgiveness of sins in the sense of a new beginning. That our life in spite of the sin of collaboration with existing forces can have significance, that liberation is possible, can be realized only in conversion. No one, however, can do it all alone; the act is destroyed as soon as it appears as solitary and private.

Liberation is possible only as the liberation of all. In *The Brothers Karamazov* Dostoevsky tells a story that moves the theme of forgiveness toward this "political" context, in the broad sense of the term.

> It's like this. Once upon a time there was a peasant woman and a very wicked woman she was. And she died and did not leave a single good deed behind. The devils caught her and plunged her into the lake of fire. So her guardian angel stood and wondered what good deed of hers he could remember to tell to God; "she once pulled up an onion in her garden," said he, "and gave it to a beggar woman." And God answered: "You take that onion then, hold it out to her in the lake, and let her take hold and be pulled out. And if you can pull her out of the lake, let her come to Paradise, but if the onion breaks, then the woman must stay where she is." The angel ran to the woman and held out the onion to her; "Come," said he, "catch hold and I'll pull you out." And he began cautiously pulling her out. He had just pulled her right out, when the other sinners in the lake, seeing how she was being drawn out, began catching hold of her so as to be pulled out with her. But she was a very wicked woman and she began kicking them. "I'm to be pulled out, not you.

It's my onion, not yours." As soon as she said that, the onion broke. And the woman fell into the lake and she is burning there to this day. So the angel wept and went away.[5]

This story speaks of an anxiety that destroys life. The old woman lives without relation to other persons. Only at one single trifling point has her life been open for others. Life for her is what she possesses privately and individually. "It's my onion, not yours." Having is for her the most important category. In having, men set themselves apart; in having they ground their privileges. Even the possible forgiveness of sins is for the woman a privilege that she must grab hold of and defend with all her might. She attempts to come to terms with the God "from above." But even the proffered deliverance does not change the course of her life, which consists of having, being afraid, securing herself, grabbing hold, beating others. That we move from having to trampling is perfectly consistent; thereby our concentration on the one goal, on redemption, is lost. The old woman "forgets" to look at the angel and to let him pull her out; she turns in the opposite direction and concentrates on the privilege, on her anxious and aggressive attempts to retain it. Thus she herself breaks the onion, because she grabs hold of it and tramples the others. Her will is divided; she wants forgiveness, but because she wants it only for herself, she destroys it, as is characteristic of evil.

Everything that we grab hold of and cling to means death. Life destroys itself wherever it is based on having, on privileges over against those who have nothing. Because we grab hold of it, it perishes. There can be no forgiveness

5. Fyodor Dostoevsky, *The Brothers Karamazov*, trans. Constance Garnett (New York: Random House, 1948), p. 367.

for one individual only. Whenever it is sought in the immediate experience of God—behind the backs of other men
and without the laborious detour through the world—it
destroys itself: the onion breaks.

Dostoevsky's story arises out of an existential thinking,
and it does not immediately raise political impulses and
questions. But it does point out very clearly the necessary
bridge from existentialist to political interpretation. As long
as life continues to be grounded and secured in the privilege of having, it destroys itself. Life is life only when
everyone belongs to it with equal right and with equal
share. To speak in images: The more that others hang onto
the old woman, the more unbreakable the tender little
onion becomes. If grabbing hold means death, then sharing
and communication mean life. No one can save himself
alone and no one is forgiven alone, if forgiveness is taken
seriously in the sense of being born anew.

"JESUS WANTS US TO BE FRIENDS"

But how does that happen? To experience the forgiveness
of sins, we need a group of human beings who make it
possible for us to begin afresh; at the very least we need
partners who accept us as we are, who have faith in our
repentance, who believe we are capable of conversion. In
the ancient church this social role was filled by the Christian community, which criticized and absolved the individual. But where do we find comparable groups in the
Christian church today? Is there not rather a deep mistrust
of giving my neighbor power over my conscience and of
allowing the group to exercise the right of judgment over
the individual? It is out of the fear of making ourselves

dependent on others that we appeal to God as absolute Lord and link our forgiveness and conversion to him alone. But can there be a nonsocial forgiveness? Critics delight in charging that the "theology of neighborliness" is banal because it does not include damnation and judgment, and therefore does not translate the *deus absconditus* into the relations of men with each other. Reflection on a forgiveness that is accomplished here "below" resolves this difficulty: damnation in fact occurs even here, consisting in the total isolation of the individual for whom a new beginning is no longer believed to be a possibility. In Germany those who have become aware of their sin from experiences in the Nazi era have scarcely any chance of conversion if they are alone. They cannot be assured by the forgiveness granted to them, for example, by a pastor, because their consciousness of sin is more serious than could be resolved in our nonobligatory forms of church life.

Conversion is more than forgiveness because it includes the future. Our world obstructs the possibility of conversion, for its principles include the isolation of men from each other and their segregation according to privilege. People live as much as possible in small, intimate units; they organize their work in terms of meaningless and unrelated fragments, and their needs are reduced to those of the consumer. Pressure to achieve, built-in competition, loneliness and inability to communicate, and insistence on privileges are characteristic of a society in which we are not permitted to make a mistake or at least not to admit it. It is a society in which conversion is excluded.

The power of the gospel is manifest in the fact that around itself it crystallizes groups that oppose and annul

such forces—at once for themselves, potentially for all. The
liberation of all, which is the intention of the gospel, sus-
pends the isolation of modern capitalism. "Jesus wants us to
be friends"—thus runs the first sentence in the Catechism
of the Community of Isolotto.[6] Thus in the groupings of
men established by the gospel the theistic, private meaning
of forgiveness of sins will become superfluous, because forgiveness has once again become a possibility in the common
life. There is a turning away from isolation and from
thoughts of achievement, and the experiences that men
have with the gospel of liberation can be talked about.

The difficulty and the future task of a political theology
consists in speaking appropriately of the gospel. This does
not mean that we could bracket out the "icy stream"
(Bloch) of Christian faith, or that we cease to preach the
law simply because it is law, or that we cease to point out
how sin functions today and what causes it outwardly and
inwardly and again outwardly. Without this kind of law
there is no gospel, and the difficulty with a new language
for the gospel has nothing to do with omitting the law or
tempering it a bit. What is involved, however, is giving a
political interpretation of the New Being, which I do not
enjoy for myself alone; what is involved is giving credibility
to the possibility of liberation from oppressive structures;
what is involved is the inducement-model for becoming
truly human. Thus, so it appears to me, theological theory
offers less help than the strengthening of faith experienced
in the present-day *communio sanctorum*. Helder Camara,

6. *Die Botschaft Jesu in Isolotto: Der Katechismus des Don Mazzi*
(Mainz/Munich. Chr. Kaiser/Matthias–Grünewald, 1969), p. 41.

Martin Luther King, or Don Mazzi bring liberation to those who see them and hear of them.

That God loves all of us and each and every individual is a universal theological truth, which without translation becomes the universal lie. The translation of this proposition is world-transforming praxis. It needs a degree of concreteness, without which it remains empty. But at the same time this proposition necessarily transcends every concrete manifestation and has neither been exhausted not rendered invalid in its translations. We have in it a greater claim than is fulfilled at any given time, a deeper want than is satisfied. Thus it focuses our attention on the fact that the concrete reality represented by our own life has begun and still bears the translation of the love of God, which we are. The letter of Christ that we ourselves are is further written (2 Cor. 3:3) and further received and read. There is no other letter capable of replacing the letter of Christ that we are.